P9-ARC-579

F R O N T I E R

evidence that others had been there both before and after them. The shortest, although often the stormiest, route across the Atlantic was from Ireland to Iceland, which was but six hundred miles, thence to Greenland, scarcely two hundred miles further, and then another six hundred miles to Labrador. This was the route followed by the gray geese in their yearly migrations, and the one Irish hermits had followed to Iceland, where they arrived some sixty years before the first Norsemen. That Irish priests awaited them on the shore when they came in to land is told in the Norse sagas. If one accepts the story of St. Brendan, the Irish went even further, perhaps to the coast of America.

Which brings me back to my original point. Nobody was *looking* for America. Early mariners and fishermen did not keep records. They went where the fish were, and when they made their catch they went ashore on the nearest available bit of land to smoke or dry the fish so they would not spoil on the return voyage. If there was land and fuel, they cared not in the least where they were. In Iceland they would have talked of their experiences, and Columbus would have believed they had landed on the shores of Tartary, proving what he wished to believe.

Although Columbus cannot be credited with the discovery of America, he was certainly responsible for its being opened to development.

It has been said a discovery or invention is not important unless made at the right time and with the right amount of fanfare. Robert Fulton was at least the eighteenth man to operate a steamboat successfully, but who gets the credit?

Nobody wanted to discover America, and so nobody paid much attention to what had been previously discovered. Columbus's successful voyage came at a time when the wars with the Moors had ended and Ferdinand and Isabella found themselves with a large army of professional fighting men who fought not for glory but for wealth. Accustomed to making their fortunes with a sword, they were looking about for new worlds to conquer. These soldiers represented a time bomb with a sputtering fuse, to which the discovery of America provided the answer. From their ranks or others like them came the men who made history in the New World—Pizarro, Cortés, Alvarado, Coronado, Balboa, De Soto, Cabeza de Vaca, and many others.

Although the voyage of Columbus was a long one for its time, many others had been made and were being made that were equally long and dangerous. Cheng Ho, a eunuch attached to the imperial court of China had made five voyages to Africa from China before the Columbus voyage. The first of these was made in 1405. Among other things Cheng Ho brought back from Africa was a giraffe, the first ever seen in China.

The Rig-Veda, one of the oldest literary documents, records many voyages upon deep water, and Dr. Sayce believed that commerce by sea had been carried on as early as 3000 B.C., when Ur-Bagas, ruler in Ur of the Chaldees, was in power. According to Professor Lacouperie, in *Western Origins of Chinese Civilization*, maritime trade between India and China began as early as 680 B.C. Colonists from India had settled in South Vietnam, Thailand, and Indonesia shortly after the time of Christ.

Columbus and the conquistadores who followed after were obviously men of courage and determination. They opened the New World to discovery and development, beginning a new chapter in the history of the world.

---

pages 16-17: Locust grove near salt pond; Cape Cod National Seashore, Massachusetts.
page 18: Tidal marsh in Bogue Sound, North Carolina.

FOUNDING A COLONY

Pioneering in America had many aspects that had nothing to do with covered wagons, gold rushes, or cattle ranching. Most of us know the stories of the settling of Virginia in 1607 and of the landing of the Pilgrims in 1620. Fewer know of the founding of New Amsterdam, which became New York, or that Santa Fe is an older city than Boston. Yet efforts to establish colonies in America began within a few years after the voyages of Columbus.

Two interesting stories, set far apart in distance as well as time, illustrate what was taking place. The first of these involved the establishment of a colony on the Delaware River by the Swedes; the second, the settling of an area called English Prairie, in Illinois. The two stories bear little resemblance to one another, but they exemplify what could and did happen.

The Hollanders had begun to trade with the Indians no later than 1610, and in 1613 they built a trading post at what is now Albany, New

York. Shortly after, William Usselinx, a Hollander, approached King Gustavus Adolphus of Sweden with the idea of creating a trading company. Efforts to raise money for the project were underway when King Gustavus died, and for a time it seemed likely the project would die with him.

Peter Minuit, who had been dismissed from the Dutch service in America because of management disagreements, came to Sweden and carried on with the effort to establish a New Sweden in America.

Count Axel Oxenstierna, chancellor for the young Swedish queen, Christina, moved quickly to get the project started, and Peter Minuit was despatched with two ships, people, provisions, and ammunition to settle in America. Their first act upon arrival was to purchase land from the Indians.

After a brief landing at what he called Paradise Point, Minuit settled his people and built Fort Christina at what is now Wilmington, Delaware. The country was unoccupied at the time, although Hollanders had moved in on the opposite side of the river.

The Dutch were angered by the arrival of the Swedes, but were not in a strong enough position to do more than protest at the time. The Swedes settled, established farms, built some modest forts at other sites, and began to adapt themselves to the country. The Dutch liked none of it, but waited until their own strength was sufficient to move against the young colony.

The Indians were discontented and required frequent presents in order to maintain peace. Under Governor Printz the Swedish colony continued to prosper, but troubles continued to grow. There was rivalry with both the Dutch and the English, the latter invading what the Swedes and Dutch considered their province to seek for furs or trade with the Indians. At Manhattan the Dutch were in a state of almost continual war, according to the word received by the Swedes, and had lost several hundred people in battles with the Indians.

The colony, established in 1638, finally came to an end when the

page 20: Church in Jamestown Festival Park, Virginia.
page 21: Powhatan Creek, Colonial National Historical Park, Virginia.

Dutch, having grown strong at New Amsterdam, moved against the Swedes with seven ships and a force of nearly seven hundred men in 1655. The Swedes were forced to surrender, and most of them were returned to Sweden, although a few elected to remain with the Dutch. Sweden was at war in Europe during much of this time and unable to support her almost forgotten colony in America.

Despite the usual emphasis on the fur trade, the Swedish colony had moved to become self-supporting, planting crops of maize, as well as other grains, and were according to reports "well supplied with meat and drink."

Those who elected to remain prospered under the Dutch and later under British rule, but never lost their loyalty to the mother country, sending to Sweden for ministers to preach the gospel and for books printed in their own language. A letter requesting ministers and books was signed by thirty persons and was laid before the king, who forwarded it to Suebilius, archbishop of Uppsala.

In subsequent years the Swedes intermarried with both the Dutch and the English, and many of their descendants are among the oldest families of Wilmington and the Delaware shores.

The second story begins with Morris Birkbeck, accompanied by George Flower, buying land in Illinois—1440 acres each, for which they paid two dollars per acre. Birkbeck's books about the area attracted attention and several visitors who commented on the colony, the buildings, and Birkbeck himself.

English Prairie was a beautiful piece of land lying near the Wabash River, but as in all such cases it needed development and improvement, and the first buildings were of necessity built in haste. Some of Birkbeck's visitors did not seem to realize this and wrote disparagingly of the entire project.

Nevertheless, others came to join him, one of these being John Woods, who describes Wanborough, Birkbeck's settlement, as "25 cabins, a tavern, a store or two, and several lodging houses." Nearby was Flower's village, comparable in size.

Kaskaskia, which had been settled more than one hundred years before, was not far away and a considerable town. The French had been the first whites to establish themselves in Illinois, and out of their settlements comes a fascinating tale that I have never found mentioned in American histories.

Before the Louisiana Territory was sold to the United States a number of French Canadians were living along the Illinois River and its vicinity. There was a Spanish garrison in the area, but the Spanish concerned themselves with nothing outside the perimeter of the fort.

It was wild country, with deer, bear, beaver, and occasional buffalo, as well as nuts, berries, and other wild fruit. It was a rich and lovely country, suited to the French Canadian way of life, and they, woodsmen of roving dispositions, had settled down there.

They were a free-living, lawless lot, by and large, good men in the woods and trustworthy, yet quick to resent an injury. The cession of the territory by Spain did not please them, and they were expected to settle down and obey the laws or leave the country. They chose to leave.

Taking what gear they could carry, they started westward, following the course of the Missouri River. There had been, in Illinois, at least 300 of these French Canadians. How many made the westward trek is not known, except that it was more than 150 men and women and some children, and more than likely half again that number, for usually only the men (the warriors) were counted.

Arriving in the west, most of them seem to have located themselves among friendly Indians in Idaho and eastern Oregon and Washington. When one allies himself with a tribe of Indians one immediately becomes the enemy of their enemies, and the story is that most of the French were killed in wars between tribes, singled out for attack because of their marksmanship.

By 1809, according to David Thompson, the Canadian explorer, only twenty-five were left, and two of these served as guides to his expedition. When these men were killed in a battle between the Salish Indians, with whom they had been living, and the Piegans, they were said to be the last of the Illinois Frenchmen.

Thompson, one of the greatest western explorers, found the two men, Michel Bordeau and Augustin Kinville, to be reliable and trustworthy, as well as excellent guides into some of the roughest country in the west. They were killed in 1812.

Certainly, the first settlers in Illinois, as well as in Indiana, Ohio, and Kentucky, had to put up with primitive conditions and inadequate buildings until they could find the time to build in a more permanent way. The people themselves were far from being primitives; they came, by and large, from the better class of farmers and craftsmen, who

Typical of the rivers and prairies encountered by early colonists:
above: Open prairie, Illinois.
page 26: Ausable River, Adirondack Mountains, New York.

sought in America the freedom from class restraints they could not find in the old country.

Birkbeck, a successful farmer in England, had a classical education. Richard Flower was also an educated man. He comments in one of his letters: "Many of us brought out ample libraries of our own, and we also had a standing library in our little town; which is supplied with newspapers and periodical publications."

The farmers in the area, whether of English, Dutch, or French ancestry, were one and all experienced, with considerable knowledge in the field.

The land they found was striking, much of it small prairies surrounded by patches of woodland, or in some cases dense forest of tall, handsome trees that extended for miles, broken only by occasional streams. There were Indians and the remains of other Indians; hunters and farmers were constantly coming upon places that gave evidence of previous settlement, and a few of the farmers gathered from their fields fragments of pottery, arrowheads, and spearheads or came upon signs of ancient campfires.

When the first settlers came, the grass grew in many places as high as the wheels on their wagons. In early spring the meadows were abloom with wild flowers, and a good farmer need only have seen what grew about him to know this was ideal for crops. Above all, there was game enough to keep a family alive until a crop could be harvested.

It was a country to attract a steady, hardworking people who expected to make their living from the land. Illinois, Iowa, and the areas immediately around them attracted the usual number of wandering hunters who drifted farther west as the country began to be settled, while those who remained built on their love of school, church, and local government.

The Illinois Indians received respect from no one, Indian or white. They had suffered severely from raids by the Iroquois, and this may have led to demoralization. There were good men among them, but according to all who knew the tribe itself they were weak, timid, and treacherous.

The murder of Chief Pontiac by an Illinois Indian led to their virtual extinction.

We have only begun to scratch at the surface of the prehistoric record of the early inhabitants of Illinois, and such digs may eventually be among the greatest tourist attractions of the area.

T H E   P I O N E E R S

Pioneering was simple at first. A man alone or with his family would move into the deep woods and if possible find a place near water or at least a spring. There they would fell trees, build a cabin, and plow the ground between the stumps.

The first settlers had built of mud and wattles as they had in the old country, and just how the log cabin came into being is a question. Some would have it that the idea came from Swedish settlers in Delaware, but Detroit, founded by the French, was largely built of logs at a time when it was unlikely the French could have known what the Swedes were doing.

The forest floor was shadowed and dark, for little sunlight penetrated the leafy canopy overhead, and among the trees there was little or no underbrush. Walking through the forest was like walking the aisles of an enormous cathedral, with the dark columns of the tree trunks rising high above.

Unless a wind was blowing or rain falling a hunter could walk for miles under these trees in absolute silence, rarely getting even the smallest glimpse of the sky. Despite the lack of underbrush, concealment was easy because of the many tree trunks and their size. A woodsman or an Indian could flit like a shadow among these trees, scarcely to be seen by either animal or man.

These early pioneers were hunters rather than farmers, and had become so of necessity. The early arrivals knew nothing of hunting and little of fishing, and few had experience in planting. The first settlers in Virginia were gentry or artisans. The former had no plans to work at all, and the latter were unskilled in what was necessary at the time.

Those who became hunters were usually of the second or third generation, boys who had grown up on the edge of wild country and had learned from or copied the Indians. There was money in furs, which could be had by trading with the Indians or by trapping, and meat was always a necessity.

The pioneers who moved into the great forest lived largely by hunting. It took time to fell the trees, clear the ground, and build a cabin. The first crops were planted among the stumps of the trees felled for the house, and farming began with a kitchen garden and cornfields.

Like the Long Hunters, these people learned to live on the outer fringe, depending on no one and wanting no interference from church or state. The ties that bound people together were loosening, new viewpoints were developing, and those who lived in the wilderness found less need for trade with the old country. The very independence of such people was planting the seeds of separation, coupled with their realization that their problems were simply not understood by their English overlords.

Those who remained on the Atlantic shores looked back with nostalgia to the old country and old country ways. Their clothing, dishes, furniture, and books were imported, and their strong sentimen-

page 28: Autumn; Kancamagus Pass, White Mountains, New Hampshire.
page 29: Open prairie; Allegheny National Forest, Pennsylvania.

tal attraction was constantly being renewed by ships arriving from England. On the frontier such contacts were rare and often abrasive.

Europeans traveling in rural areas expected subservience but found an irritating independence, failing to understand that what they were encountering was a new sort of man. Europe had for hundreds of years been a relatively settled society, changing slowly and according to patterns known and accepted. Such was not the case on the frontier. The pioneer had to constantly adapt to changing conditions or to peace or war with various tribes of Indians. He not only considered himself as good as any man but had proved it under the harshest conditions.

Europeans traveling in the back country often found themselves treated rudely or with indifference. Dismounting at a tavern, they rarely saw anyone come forward to take a horse to the stable or carry their luggage inside. When some bystander was asked to take a horse to the stable, he more often than not would either stare with contempt or reply with some rude comment. For the most part men stabled their own horses on the frontier and took care of their own gear.

Horses were few until the later years. At first men traveled by foot or by canoe, but once over the mountains the rivers flowed west, and the Ohio, the Beautiful River, was the favored avenue of exploration. Men and families settled along its banks, pushing steadily westward until suddenly they found themselves facing the Great Plains, which some called the Great American Desert.

The methods of pioneering that had come into being in the century past were suddenly no longer valid. There were no trees on the Great Plains that could be used in building a cabin, barns, sheds, and whatever else was needful. Moreover, the country was too open. It worried people accustomed to the comparative shelter of the forest, and for a time pioneering ceased except for the few hunters who pushed on into the plains to explore, meet Indians of a different sort, and hunt the wild game.

The French, pushing down from the Great Lakes, were among the first to venture into the plains country, and the Spanish had ventured east from their settlements in and around Santa Fe.

Others had been pushing into the midcontinent area by one means or another. In 1698 two ships commanded by a Captain Barr and financed by Daniel Coxe sailed up the Mississippi for some distance. It is probable they also ventured into the Missouri. In the

Palmer-Epard cabin; Homestead National Monument, Nebraska.

early 1700s a Frenchman named Derbanne sailed up that river for a considerable distance, possibly as far as the Mandan area.

When the pioneers began to move into the plains they lived in dugouts cut from hillsides or riverbanks, only later beginning to build sod houses.

Often these were built against a bank or cut into a hill to offer added security and warmth. In later years when the roofs became green with grass it was not at all unusual for a buffalo bull to wander out onto the roof and have it collapse under him.

Sod houses could be warm and snug. Often when visitors were expected the earth floor would be sprinkled with water and tamped hard; then with a small stick or other instrument a design would be traced, resembling a carpet. The design would not last long but would, for the first comers at least, add a pretty touch to the bleak surroundings.

Many sod houses were built on the open prairie and roofed with plank bought in the nearest town that could provide such things.

Slowly the pioneers moved into Nebraska, Kansas, and the Dakotas, plowing the earth, planting crops, fighting grasshoppers, drouth, flood, and all the other evils that could beset a settler in wild country. Social life centered around the church when there was one, but at first two or three settlers' families would meet at the house of one or the other, and if there was a fiddle there would be dancing.

Dancing, however, was frowned upon in some quarters, and never took place if the preacher was present. Usually, social occasions were limited to eating and conversation, the women in one group, the men in another. On the part of the men the conversation was largely of the land, the weather, crops, and politics. The women talked of their homes, how they coped with problems, their children, and the new neighbors, if any.

Often cattle herds from Texas would pass through, and a settler would try to get them to bed down near his home, for when they departed they would leave a healthy deposit of cow chips that when dried by the sun made excellent fuel. Others did not want the cattle near them at all, for they ate pasture that the farmer himself needed. Yet by the time the settlers were scattered over the prairie the days of the cattle drives were drawing to a close.

The settling of the west had many aspects, and the picture was by no means uniform. From the first, aside from the individual colonists, there were numerous groups who crossed the ocean and came west

together, establishing colonies of their own and working together as a community.

The lawlessness in western communities has been much over-rated because of its dramatic aspects. The stories of outlaws and badmen are exciting, and western men themselves still love to relate them. However, over most of the west schools and churches had come with the first settlers, and law accompanied them. The gunfighters and cardsharps were on the wrong side of the tracks, most of them unknown to the general run of the population, although they might be pointed out on occasion.

From the beginning there was a sense of order, a need for local, county, and state governments, and the citizens took an active hand in what was being done. Politics in most western communities was not the business of the few, but of all, and most men were well informed on the local politics, if not the international. The general feeling was to avoid foreign entanglements, as Washington had suggested, and get on with building a nation.

The building was not done by a few selected persons; it was done by the people, a people who knew what they wanted and how to get it.

page 34: Sod homestead; Oglala National Grassland, Nebraska.
above: Tionesta Creek, Tionesta Scenic Preserve, Allegheny National Forest,
    Pennsylvania.

THE LONG HUNTERS

They came to the mountains in the springtime of their years, following the Warrior's Path into what is now Tennessee, and they found no people there.

The land lay empty and still. Green meadows, wide and beautiful rivers lying comfortably in the folds of the hills, but no campfires, no villages.

Yet there were ghosts, for the Mound Builders had lived here, and those mysterious white people driven off or killed by the Cherokee or the Shawnee. The evidence favors the Cherokee, but two tribes telling the same story is no mystery. Such things have happened many times, resulting from the capture of a woman from one tribe by another and her telling her native stories to her children. After a generation or two the origin of the story is forgotten.

There was game in abundance, and the evidence of even more game from times long gone. They found the big bones around the salt

licks, and the tusks of mammoth or mastodon. There were buffalo, several varieties of deer, bear, and much else, including fur-bearing animals that promised quick returns.

De Soto had passed through a part of the area, and Juan Pardo explored further, the former in 1541, the latter in 1567.

Who else came early to the land we cannot be sure, for many left no records. William Byrd speaks of Virginia traders among the Cherokee as early as 1612, but even they were not the first. The wild country and the mountains were a challenge that could not be ignored. Where there is unknown country there are always men who wish to see what awaits them there, and someone is always pushing a little further.

There was no assurance as to how they would be treated by Indians. Much depended on the mood of the group encountered. Men were killed without warning; others sat through what seemed to be a friendly meal only to be slain at the end of it. Yet in other cases they were escorted to the village, fed, entertained, and returned to their settlements.

The Long Hunters were so called because they followed long trails for a long time. They were dreamers and doers, these men of the Long Hunt, in the wilderness for months on end, returning—if they did return—with huge packs of furs and tales of the wild and beautiful country they had seen. In much of Tennessee and Kentucky they found no one. Here or there they might come upon the ashes of an old campfire, for Indians did hunt the land upon occasion.

Why such a lovely land was deserted is a mystery, a mystery that may be connected with rumors of white men. One story is that of Prince Madoc of Wales, who is believed to have established a colony in the 1170s. Sheets of copper, axes, hoes, and other utensils of metal have been found in the area. Usually the story is dismissed as myth, but there is considerable evidence on both sides of the Atlantic.

This is Daniel Boone country, but for all that great hunter accomplished, he was a latecomer.

page 36: Cumberland Falls on the Cumberland River, Kentucky.
page 37: Ash Cave, Hocking Hills State Park, Ohio.
pages 38-39: Pinnacle Overlook, Cumberland Gap National Historical Park, Tennessee-Kentucky-Virginia border.

Batts and Fallam traveled some of the region in 1671, and James Needham led a small group in 1673. Among them was a lad named Gabriel Arthur, whom Needham left among the Indians to learn their language. Needham started to return to report to Colonel Abraham Wood, who had sent him out. En route he was killed by an Indian of his own party. The same Indian tried to have young Arthur killed as well. Actually bound to a stake to be burned, he was saved when an old chief objected.

Gabriel Arthur spent a year among the Indians, traveling with them to Florida and exploring much of what is now Kentucky. A friendly chief returned him to Fort Henry and Colonel Wood in May of 1674. Arthur had spent a year among the Indians wandering over country largely unknown to white men, as far as we know.

Martin Chartier, who had been with La Salle, traded in somewhat the same area in 1679 and 1680. Tonti, who had been La Salle's second in command, told of "Carolina adventurers" on the Ohio and the Tennessee in 1686, and Jean Couture traveled the length of the Tennessee River in 1696.

All of this occurred approximately one hundred years before Daniel Boone, Elisha Walden, and their like blazed their own trails west of Cumberland Gap.

At least two dozen more could be listed who wandered the Kentucky-Tennessee country in the years before Boone. How many there were of whom we know nothing may only be surmised, as such men are not inclined to keep records and undoubtedly many could not write.

Research and my own wanderings have made me very wary of "discoverers," for almost invariably somebody was there before them. The man who considered himself the "first" would find initials carved on a tree or runes scratched on a rock to prove others had preceded him.

As for the Long Hunters, had it not been for the need of ammunition some might never have returned at all. The country into which they ventured was rich with wild game, edible plants, and fish leaping from streams. The Long Hunter was only secondarily an explorer, so he often lingered for weeks in some likely spot where the fishing was good and life comparatively easy. Our present conception of the importance of time (born in part from the railroad timetable) had not come into being. People lived and worked by the sun's rising and setting, and when they paid attention at all, they judged longer periods by the waxing and waning of the moon.

Yet from time to time they did return to sell their furs, lay in fresh supplies of the little they needed, and tell their stories.

These men traveled as the Indian did, on foot or by canoe. The birchbark canoe, so well known from the stories of James Fenimore Cooper, was not generally available. Some Indians had only dugouts made from hollowed logs, much heavier and more difficult to handle than the bark canoe.

There were paths, most of them created originally by buffalo, (there were many buffalo east of the Appalachians before the coming of the white man) that were used by Indian war parties or traders. Naturally these paths were used by the Long Hunters as well, although they usually disappeared into the deep woods very promptly when Indians appeared. Indians and white men traveled on foot, often running at an easy pace that would carry them many miles in a day. Horses did not come to those paths until much, much later, and then they were more often than not used as pack animals.

The white man in America had much to learn from the Indian, who knew the land and its ways from long experience. On the other hand, the white man brought with him many items the Indian could get in only one of two ways: by trade or war. In the one hundred and eighty years from the first settlements until we became a nation, all the patterns of relationship between the Indian and the white man had already become established.

The Long Hunter, living far from his own kind, could exist only by being better than the Indian at the Indian's way of living. Many did not succeed. As the Indians were in a constant state of warfare with each other, a white man who became friends with one tribe or nation immediately became an enemy of their enemies, whether he wished it so or not.

The French established an early relationship with the Hurons, who controlled the fur trade on the Great Lakes and the upper St. Lawrence River. This automatically made them the enemy of the Iroquois, who became allied with the British. This alliance persisted until after the American Revolution, and much of the bloodiest fighting on the frontier in that war was with England's Iroquois allies.

South of the Tennessee River was Cherokee country, a people who absorbed into the tribe several Scotch and Irish traders of better than average intelligence. Some of these men, notably James Adair, had a profound influence on the Cherokee future.

The Long Hunters were men who had begun learning their trade as boys hunting meat for the family. They were born with rifles in their hands, and they learned to live off the country as Indians did. Often they came of pioneer families who had pushed into the big woods beyond the settlements, and so developed the woodsman's skills from boyhood.

Education is of many kinds, and these boys went to school with Nature, learning to read a trail as a modern man would read his newspaper, and reading the forest itself just as well, knowing its plants and animals, the ways of the insects and of birds, and where to find springs. Many of the girls could have done as well had they been called upon, and there were some who proved it in escaping from Indians. At a later time Annie Oakley became famous for her shooting, her skill acquired in just that way, but in an earlier time there were girls in every hollow who could have done as well or nearly as well. Marksmanship was not a pastime or an entertainment, it was necessary for survival.

The Long Hunters made their own clothing from the skins of animals they killed, and their own moccasins. These wore out rather quickly and were continually being replaced or, occasionally, repaired. A few even made their own gunpowder, and, of course, all molded their own bullets. Usually bars of lead were carried along, but deposits of lead were sometimes known and used.

They were blazing another trail, unbeknownst to themselves, for they had freed themselves from the need for many of the trappings of what was called civilization. They were sufficient unto themselves and did not need the many things that shops had to offer. They did not need importations from abroad; in other words, they did not need the old country. Here was another seed ground of the Revolution, another aspect of independence.

---

page 42: Moonset; Lake Como, Bitteroot Range, Montana.
page 45: Blackwater Falls State Park, West Virginia.

44

THE MAINE ISLANDS

A storyteller could devote a lifetime to the Maine islands, and when he shipped his oars for the last time the ghosts would chuckle at how little he knew.

It is interesting to speculate on who came first to these shores. Indians, perhaps, but what Indians? The Red Paint people were the most advanced of all until the coming of the white man 4,000 years later, and judging by the evidence of their catches they were fine deep-water fishermen, but they were not the first.

No doubt many came and departed leaving few indications behind and making almost no impression. There is a school of thought that believes any arrival from the outside results in culture shock, but such is not the case. Researching among southern Indians, for example, one finds little evidence that De Soto's march across the south from Florida to the Mississippi had any more effect than the passing of a small cloud across the sun. A few years later they were forgotten, as was Coronado after his brief foray into the plains. 47

page 46: Polished bedrock; Schoodic Peninsula, Acadia National Park, Maine.
page 47: Somes Sound, Acadia National Park, Maine.
above: Bass Harbor Head, Acadia National Park, Maine.
page 49: Otter Point, Acadia National Park, Maine.

The Maine islands are America's outposts in the Atlantic, the first land to be seen, with inviting anchorages and the promise of fresh water and fuel.

Monhegan looms against the sky, visible on a good day from fifty miles at sea. There is a possibility that St. Brendan landed here in 565 A.D., and there is evidence of Viking landings five hundred years later. John Cabot was here in 1497, Verrazano in 1524, and Gomez a year later.

Thevet, Gosnold, Weymouth, and Champlain also visited Monhegan, and in after years, if not before, there were Breton, Norman, Basque, and British fishermen who came to smoke and dry their catches before the long voyage home.

In 1614 Captain John Smith visited the island on a voyage of exploration and mapmaking, and left an interesting account of his stay.

A rarely reported outpost was established by a Captain Damerill at Damerils Isles sometime before 1614. This was later known as Damerilscove, and in 1622 thirty ships were fishing out of there. Both the Virginia colony and that established by the Pilgrims came here for supplies, and there were many ships among the islands from the time of Cabot.

Long before this time Irish seamen had sailed the northern seas in their coracles, boats made of several thicknesses of cowhide that were excellent seagoing craft. The coracle, like the Chinese seagoing junk, sailed atop the water rather than through it, like a duck rather than a fish. The Irish used their coracles in trade with England, Brittany, and Spain, and they were known to have visited many of the northern islands, including Iceland, where the first Vikings found them waiting on the beach to welcome them.

With all the seafaring that was taking place along the Atlantic shores of Europe and Africa it would be amazing if some of those ships had not crossed the ocean. The point is, as I have said elsewhere, that nobody cared.

The islands of Maine are singularly beautiful, each with its distinct character, and the first arrivals found the larger islands heavily wooded, many of the trees of excellent material for masts or yards, which were constantly needful of repair or replacement. There were lovely beaches of sand, picturesque cliffs, and weirdly shaped rocks. Indians had lived on or visited most of the islands, and the seas about swarmed with fish, so it was no wonder that fishing stations were established here before the more publicized colonies at Virginia in 1607 and Plymouth in 1620.

Much credit is due Captain John Smith for his mapping of these islands and his recognition of their importance.

T H E   F O R E S T

Trees can exist without man, but it is doubtful if man could continue to exist upon this planet without trees.

Trees remove carbon dioxide from the atmosphere and give back oxygen, their root systems hold water upon the land, and their leaves discharge water into the atmosphere. An acre of trees will process hundreds of tons of water each month, yet we have been stripping away our great forests at an amazing rate, with no apparent thought for the future. Nor can we plead ignorance. The facts have been published over and over again.

Each patch of woodland has its own personality, and no two are exactly alike. Trees and other plants are like people and wild animals, for they will invade any area where there is a chance of survival, with their root systems protecting the soil from runoff and stabilizing mountainsides and hillsides.

Someday man may invent a machine as perfect as a tree that

page 50: Birch and maple; Adirondack Mountains, New York.
page 51: Autumn flow in Lost River Gorge, White Mountains, New Hampshire.
above: Balsam fir on Mount Mitchell, North Carolina.

absorbs sunlight and turns it into food. Other plants also do this, of course, but I think none with the efficiency of trees or in the quantity of the forest.

To walk into the forest is to walk into quietness. The sounds are small sounds, whispering sounds—leaves brushing, branches rubbing against one another, the scurry of a squirrel or a woodmouse. Long ago in Minnesota, not far from where the Mississippi begins at Lake Itasca, I decided to walk around a small lake. I was twelve years old and had come from a prairie state where the only trees lay along the rivers or in tree claims. The walk I was attempting would be something like three miles, but on the far side of the lake opposite my uncle's home there was no trail, and over much of the distance the trees grew right to the water's edge. To keep from becoming lost I had to work my way through the forest within sight of the lake.

Soon I was deep in the forest, and the further I went the more I began to think of bears. There were occasional black bears, I had heard, but I put them out of mind and began working my way through the brush, climbing over deadfalls, ducking under low branches, pushing my way through thick stands of brush, imagining myself a character from James Fenimore Cooper.

The silence was absolute but for the sounds of my own passage. From time to time I paused to listen, as one will. Out on the lake there was the call of a loon, the loneliest sound imaginable. Through the leaves I could glimpse my uncle's house. It was no more than a few hundred yards away, but on the other side of the lake. He was gone for the afternoon and there was nobody else within miles. I was alone.

For a moment I stood listening, looking all about. There was no sound, and the brush was so thick a bear could be within a few feet without my realizing. I had been assured a bear would be as eager to avoid me as I was to avoid it, but I had little confidence in that idea.

Slowly I moved on. There was no wind among the trees. It had become very warm. I crawled over a fallen tree that was swarming with ants. I was beginning to wish I had never begun this venture, wishing I was back at the cabin, looking out over the lake and eating a biscuit, or drinking cold, clear water from the well.

Suddenly right before me was a small clearing around a magnificent Norway pine. I started forward eagerly, and then the forest floor exploded with a roar.

Scared? Of course I was scared! Right out of my wits, if I had any.

I had almost stepped on a cluster of partridges resting comfortably in the leaves, and they took off en masse. Anyone who has experienced it knows exactly what I mean, and no other birds I know of make a similar sound. There is no more startling sound in any forest, and since that day I have walked in many.

After that it was anticlimactic. Once I paused to spend a few minutes sitting and resting while I picked and ate blueberries. When I finally got back to the house my feet were dragging and I was dead beat. It was my first venture into a forest alone and my first real scare.

Forests have many ways of protecting themselves from enemies, but thus far they have no protection against man, the greatest enemy of all. Some trees, such as knobcone pines, carry out their own reforestation. Their seeds are sealed tight within hard cones, where they may lie dormant for years until the outer shell rots away or the seeds are made to pop out by the intense heat of a fire. When heat makes the cones explode, the seeds pop out, replanting the forest that has just burned. Lodgepole pines react to fire in much the same way.

Aspens may be cut down or burned, yet the roots will lie waiting for the favorable moment and then spring up again, covering a burned-off slope with fresh growth.

Much inadvertent planting of trees is done by jays and squirrels, who hide nuts in the earth and never return to claim them. Other seeds are often carried in the fur of animals who happen to brush a plant in passing. Some trees grow their cones high up or far out on branches so they will fall some distance from the parent tree.

Earlier I mentioned tree claims in speaking of the plains country. When homesteaders were allowed to claim 160 acres of land by building and living on it, they were allowed to claim another 160 acres if they would plant ten acres to trees and care for them. When I was a boy most of these trees had grown tall, adding to the beauty of the prairie country as well as forming windbreaks and convenient woodlots. The shelterbelts planted during the Roosevelt regime were a development of this idea.

Marvelous changes take place in the eastern forests, where grow so many deciduous trees that shed their leaves in the autumn. As the days grow shorter the ability of the tree to produce chlorophyll declines, and the green coloring begins to lose out to other pigments in the leaves. For a few weeks the forest becomes a place of extraordinary

Hardwoods; Tionesta Preserve, Allegheny National Forest, Pennsylvania.

beauty, then the leaves fall and the branches become bare and gray and the trees are prepared for the snow and cold weather. Spring brings another change, when suddenly the gray branches become a misty green. The buds grow quickly, the trees leaf out, and the forest is itself once more. Still later the laurel is in bloom, and the rhododendron and azalea leave the slopes awash with color.

Each area and each successive period of time has its own particular beauty to offer, and within the forest itself there is constant change. The falling of leaves and needles, the decaying of stumps and dead limbs, all add to the buildup of the soil beneath the trees. Insects and other animals and the processes of decay reduce the largest fallen tree, returning its elements to the growing strength of the earth.

page 57: Linville Falls, Blue Ridge Parkway, North Carolina.

THE SMOKIES AND
THE BLUE RIDGE

I wrote of them in my novel *To the Far Blue Mountains,* for these were the mountains that lay along the border between the known and the unknown, the mountains beyond which my character Barnabas Sackett had not traveled in the 1600s. Enchanting mountains they were, and enchanting they are, unpopulated then but for a few Indians and later peopled by Scotch, Irish, and Welsh, who were born singing. As a people they remind me of the old Greek tale of a people who discovered the joy of singing and sang until they forgot all else, even to eat. So the gods changed them into cicadas, who sing through their whole lives.

The names are poetry enough, the Nantahala Mountains, Yellow Creek, Water-Rock Knob, the Plott Balsams, Tellico Ridge, Clingman's Dome, Newfound Gap, Craggy, Grandfather, the Big Yellow, Roan Mountain and the Unakas, Humpback Mountain, Bearwallow, Crabtree, Three Knobs and Buck Creek Gap, each an invitation to wander, to go

and see for yourself, as Barnabas Sackett did and Jubal, his son, who went west and still further west.

It's a place to go *cooterin' around,* for there's always something to see, or you can sit on the porch and whittle while talking of the fishing or of the black bear Lige saw when he was crossing over by Indian Gap.

A man could spend months just discovering the coves, the balds, and some of the cabins tucked back in the folds of the hills. Some of the families who live in those cabins were here before the Revolution, and some of their ancestors may have gone down the mountain with

---

page 58: Fog-shrouded Newfound Gap, Great Smoky Mountains National Park, Tennessee-North Carolina border.

page 59: Cades Cove, Great Smoky Mountains National Park, Tennessee-North Carolina border.

above: Iced trees; Newfound Gap, Great Smoky Mountains National Park, Tennessee-North Carolina border.

page 61: Mountain laurel; Blue Ridge Mountains, Virginia.

Rhododendron and rock slabs; Blue Ridge Mountains, Virginia.

John Sevier and Isaac Shelby when they went after Captain Ferguson, to corner him at King's Mountain.

You can see the mountains in the morning with the mists upon them, and in the evening with the sunset cresting their ridges with light. Beautiful as they are one can scarcely imagine what they must have been like before the big trees were lumbered away. There were giant chestnuts then, and tulip trees a dozen feet around. Once, long ago, I worked in the lumber yards of the northwest and did some felling of trees and some topping also. Finally, I quit. I no longer wanted to help in the logging of trees it had taken hundreds of years to grow.

Yet there is wild and beautiful country still, areas where the old forest has been preserved so one can actually have some understanding of how it must have been when the first pioneers began to push back from the coast.

There are many leafy hollows, quiet, remote places, a world apart. And everywhere, the flame azaleas. The Nantahalas are a small range forming a sort of link between the Blue Ridge and the Smoky mountains, but a range unto themselves, their highest peak being Standing Indian, something less than six thousand feet. Now that isn't high by western standards (the lowest point on my Colorado ranch is a thousand feet higher), but mountains should not be judged by altitude. There are so many other factors. It is said that only one other place on earth (in China) has as great a variety of plant growth as this general area. Certainly, there are no more beautiful mountains on earth than the Southern Appalachians of which these, the Blue Ridge and the Smokies, are a part.

The Nantahala Gorge is spectacular, very deep and so narrow only the noonday sun reaches the bottom in some places. There are many legends about it. One of these says the gorge was the haunt of a monster called Ooktena, a horned dragon or serpent. A jewel gleamed from the center of its head and put a curse on any Indian who looked upon it. Finally a bold young Cherokee ventured into the gorge and killed the monster, taking the jewel, which was supposed to reveal the future to its possessor.

There are caves in the walls of the gorge that were reputed to have been inhabited by a people who preceded the Cherokees in the country.

THE OUTER BANKS

They are low, sandy islands that form a protective barrier off the coast of North Carolina. Behind them lie several sheltered sounds, the major ones being Albemarle and Pamlico. Into these a number of rivers empty their waters, and outside lies the open ocean and a region once known as the graveyard of the Atlantic.

There is some evidence that these islands or sections of them were once heavily forested, but this was followed by a period when there was low brush and small, shaggy, wind-blown trees. Buried in the sand are the ribs of wrecks, and the shifting tides bring to the surface still other evidences of bygone shipwrecks and the trunks of ancient trees.

It is a place of storm and a place of legend. Cape Hatteras is here (it was off Hatteras on a freighter bound from Galveston to England that I was first seasick), and scattered about are some pieces of New England granite, about all that is left of the first lighthouse built here. It was built at the behest of Alexander Hamilton by a distant relative of mine, General Henry Dearborn, later secretary of war under Jefferson. He built the lighthouse in the years 1796–97.

Blackbeard the pirate haunted these waters. He often took his ship into Oracoke and had friends in Edenton, and it was near here that Blackbeard was tracked down and defeated by Lieutenant Robert Maynard.

One of my favorite stories of the region is that of Theodosia Burr, daughter of Aaron Burr, once Vice-President of the United States. Born in 1783, on her mother's death in 1794 she took on the social responsibilities of her father's household. Largely educated at home by her father, she was proficient in Latin and Greek and accustomed to the society of men of business and politics. In 1801 she married Joseph Alston, who became governor of South Carolina. From 1808 until 1812 she acted as financial agent for her father, who was traveling abroad. She was sailing north to visit her father, who had just returned from Europe, when she was, according to the approved story, lost in the wreck of the *Patriot* off the North Carolina coast.

Down along the Outer Banks there are other stories. One of these is that the *Patriot* was deliberately lured into dangerous waters by lights displayed on the Outer Banks and that the ship was looted by pirates. This story says that Theodosia, along with others, was made to walk the plank to her death. Some years after, two pirates about to be executed confessed to being members of the crew that killed Theodosia, and still later a dying man in an almshouse also confessed, saying he had been haunted by the memory of the beautiful woman they had killed.

page 64: The Altoona, Cape Hatteras National Seashore, North Carolina.
page 65: Hatteras Light, Cape Hatteras National Seashore, North Carolina.
page 67: (above) Cord grass in salt marsh; Okrakoke Island, Hatteras National Seashore, North Carolina; (below) Dune grass; Jockey's Ridge State Park, North Carolina.

Yet there are other stories, one being that instead of being murdered the beautiful Theodosia was kept by the pirate captain and lived for many years on the Outer Banks or nearby. This is the story I favor, for I cannot see any pirate in his right mind destroying a young and beautiful woman, nor can I imagine Theodosia, her father's daughter, allowing herself to be forced to walk the plank. She was much too intelligent and too skilled a politician for that.

There is, of course, another story. That her mind had been shocked by the death of her son not long before, and the horrors of the shipwreck and the aftermath of murder unhinged her reason, and because of her loss of reason she was not murdered but lived on for years among the Bankers.

In her possession, according to the story, was a portrait of herself. That portrait was given to a doctor to pay for medical attention and is now in a museum.

Also on the Outer Banks is Kitty Hawk, the site where the Wright brothers made history with their first heavier-than-air flight.

This was also the home of the porpoise Hatteras Jack, whom Ripley made famous in *Believe It or Not*, for Hatteras Jack for many years guided all ships into Hatteras Inlet, every one brought safely to berth. Hatteras Jack performed the self-imposed duties for twenty years until in 1910 buoys were anchored to mark the safe passage. Jack, no longer needed, departed for parts unknown.

In several of my novels I have dealt with these waters; in *Sackett's Land*, *To the Far Blue Mountains*, and *Fair Blows the Wind*, I have written of these islands and of the sounds and the rivers behind them.

There are thousands of stories along the Outer Banks, stories of mystery, adventure, horror, and lost souls, as well as lost ships. This is, after all, on the edge of what has been called the Bermuda Triangle.

---

page 68: Sunrise; Cape Hatteras National Seashore, North Carolina.

THE BAYOUS

There are bayous, dark and moody, in Caddo Lake, Texas, in Okefenokee Swamp, Georgia and near Trussum Pond, Delaware, among other places, but when we think of bayous we think of Louisiana. When we who were reared upon the American classics think of Louisiana we think of *Evangeline.* Longfellow is not much read these days, and it is a pity, for he was both a good poet and a teller of American tales. In *Evangeline* he captured the heart of an historical event, taking few liberties with the facts. Our children miss much, I believe, in not growing up with such stories, as well as with *Rip Van Winkle* and *The Legend of Sleepy Hollow.*

Southern Louisiana is a maze of meandering streams, rivers, and natural canals that wind through the Mississippi delta and the countryside, finding their way around salt marshes and forests of cypress and live oak, all dripping with Spanish moss. More often than not, the waters of the inner bayous are dark and still, shadowed by great trees, and a pirogue moves almost without any sound but the ripple of the water as it passes.

71

The bayous are places of mystery, or so they seem, and to venture into their maze without a guide is asking for trouble. Once, when we were poling along through a dark stretch where cypress towered above us, a snowy white egret flew along above the water on slow-moving wings, a single white spot in all that shadowed stillness.

The Cajuns, descendants of the French who were unwillingly deported from their homeland Arcadia, inhabit the bayous, and only those who live among them can know them well. Storms and floods bring constant change, felling great trees, closing some channels, opening others. Many of the old bayous have become choked with water hyacinth, a plant introduced by accident which crowded in, multiplied fantastically, and now covers many bayous and ponds from side to side, leaving no openings for the sun to get through to the waters below.

Under the waters the hyacinth roots form a jungle, an overgrown, underwater forest without oxygen where fish cannot live. Every means has been tried to control the hyacinth, but without any obvious success. The manatee, imported to fight them, may be the best weapon, for they eat the hyacinths and grow fat on them. The trouble is that hunters find the manatee a good source of meat, and they are sometimes killed. Once common, they are now rarely seen.

Often I wonder if man has any more control over his migrations than do such plants as the hyacinth. Where there is opportunity it will be taken, whether by man, animal, or plant.

The bayous are many—LaFourche, Teche, Atchafalaya, Dorcheat, and many others with names known only locally. It is a curious world, more than half water, and what appears to be solid earth might give way under one's weight.

page 70: Bald cypress trunks in Caddo Lake State Park, Texas.
page 71: Sunrise in The Pocket, Okefenokee Swamp, Georgia.
page 73: Mixed plant community; Corkscrew Sanctuary, Big Cypress Swamp, Florida.

There are things to be seen: a deer splashing through a swamp, the snout of an alligator, birds of many colors and sizes. Slaves were smuggled into the country through these bayous, for the importation of slaves became illegal in 1820, a fact forgotten by many Americans. Under the Act of 1820 foreign slave trade was declared piracy. In addition to the forfeiture of their vessels the death penalty was decreed for U.S. citizens who were engaged in the importation of slaves.

Despite this, slaves were smuggled in through the bayous and sold in New Orleans.

Trappers have worked the bayou country for beaver, for muskrat, and now for nutria. However, the alligator is the nutria's greatest enemy. The nutria was not native to the area but was introduced by man and very quickly made itself at home. The white-tailed deer is common, and swamp rabbits are frequently seen. There have been reports of panthers and even of jaguars in some of the wildest parts of the delta. It has been my experience that one rarely sees a panther, or mountain lion, unless it is treed by dogs or fleeing before a fire.

74

If one has a competent guide there are few areas more beautiful than the bayou country. Those I have named are the best known, of course, some of them lined with cottages or houseboats. Others are Bayou Tellebonne, Grand Caillou, Pointe du Chien, and du Large, all worth seeing.

A Cajun in a pirogue can take you anywhere, and there are many places you will see no other way. The ones who took me around the bayous and swamps so long ago talked very little, a nod of the head or the lift of a chin to indicate something worth looking at. But back at their cottage, amongst themselves, over a bowl of turtle stew there would be much good talk.

Once it was a cottonmouth snake my Cajun guide pointed out, another time a raccoon which I was already watching. Raccoons are great fishermen, and great thieves as well, and in a place so rich in crayfish, oysters, and all manner of edible creatures and plants the raccoon lives a good life, wary only of hounds and bobcats.

There are black bears, too, although I did not see any in the bayou country. Bears, too, by all reports are usually fat here, for there is so much to eat.

Jean Lafitte, pirate, smuggler, and patriot, knew the bayous as well as any man, and used them frequently. The governor of Louisiana offered a reward for his capture at one time, and Lafitte promptly countered with a reward for the capture of the governor. He maintained, among other things, a blacksmith shop in New Orleans usually operated by his brother. But it was a place where Lafitte himself was frequently seen.

There is a story about Jean Lafitte that I like. True or not, I do not know—but it is likely to be true, for it is typical of the man. The story is that before the Battle of New Orleans, in which he and his pirates fought on the American side, Lafitte was approached in the Old Absinthe House by a British agent who offered him a handful of gold to guide British ships through the bayous to attack New Orleans. Jean Lafitte, it is said, pinned the man's hand to the bar with his knife blade, scattering the gold.

page 74: Bald cypress; Caddo Lake State Park, Texas.
pages 76-77: Bald Cypress; Trussum Pond Preserve, Delaware.

W E S T W A R D
T H E W A G O N S

Nobody had thought to mention the wind. It came from somewhere over the edge of the world and stirred the shimmering grass like the waves of the sea. It billowed the wagon tops and rattled sand against the canvas. It dried the skin to parchment and filled the air with gritty dust.

They gathered in Missouri to wait for the grass to turn green before they began their westward trek, for the grass was needed to feed their animals. Once started it was important to keep moving to reach the Sierra passes before they were closed by snow. The wiser ones, if they could afford it, would start a month earlier and feed grain to their stock until the grass was high. This enabled them to escape the mud caused by spring rains, as they could reach higher, drier country before the rains fell.

There were thousands of wagons, forever moving. The season for travel was short and there was no place for laggards. Was the whole world moving west? Would there be any gold left or any land? 79

There were sixty wagons in this train divided into platoons of fifteen each. Off to the south and scarcely a mile away there was another, somewhat smaller train, and you knew there was one ahead, for there had been signs of their passing.

Companies of fewer than ten wagons were not advised. Larger companies were rarely attacked by Indians, although there was always the risk of a quick raid to drive off the stock. This was one major reason oxen were preferred by most travelers. Horses and mules were faster but more apt to be stolen. Moreover, oxen survived better on prairie grass and required less care than either horses or mules. Also, their hoofs were better adapted to travel over western prairies, where roads were nonexistent.

Two thousand pounds was the accepted load for a westbound covered wagon; however, the usual starting load was close to twenty-five hundred pounds, with the expectation that consumption of food would lighten the load by the time rougher country was reached.

For each adult two hundred pounds of flour, thirty pounds of pilot bread, ten pounds of rice, seventy-five pounds of bacon, five pounds of coffee, two pounds of tea, half a bushel of dried beans, a bushel of dried fruit, twenty-five pounds of sugar, a half bushel of cornmeal, and some saleratus for baking. Naturally, these amounts varied with individuals and personal tastes, but every ounce needed to be calculated with care.

A small sheet-iron stove as well as a Dutch oven would be essential, and a cast iron skillet. Tin dishes were preferred because of their lighter weight. There needed to be a rifle for each adult male, powder, shot, a bullet mold, and preferably a shotgun for hunting birds and small game.

Clothing was packed, as well as extra boots and shoes. There were tools for wagon and harness repair, and a saddle horse was a necessity for hunting and for rounding up stock. Milk cows could be driven with a common herd.

Those who planned to subsist on wild game were usually disappointed, for the passing of so many wagons caused the game to drift into the further hills, far from the line of march. Those who made an early start often found game, or if hunters were willing to go far afield they might meet with success.

Buffalo rarely ranged west of South Pass, although in the years before the country was settled they were found east of the Appalachians.

page 78: Flash flood; San Mateo Mountains, New Mexico.
page 79: Oregon Trail, South Pass, Wyoming.
above: Black Rock Playa, Nevada.

Oregon Trail ruts; Wyoming.

Deer, antelope, and elk were found on the plains and along the creek bottoms, but all game tended to move away from the westward trails and into wilder country.

Such a westward journey required an average of five months, although with good stock and equipment, as well as a break in the weather conditions, this might be shortened to four. For the first ten days to two weeks of the westward trek from Missouri the train would be passing small settlements or outlying farms or cabins. There were a few stores that sold provisions, but prices were high and the supplies limited.

In moister areas west of the Missouri River bluestem grasses grew six to eight feet high. Found largely along creek bottoms they tended to disappear as the wagons moved westward into short-grass country, where buffalo grass and blue grama were the staples. The grazing was still good, and the value of oxen proved itself anew with every mile. Oxen were good rustlers and given a chance to graze could maintain themselves where a horse or mule would starve.

The trail could be half a mile wide at points, but that varied according to the terrain. The trails narrowed at river crossings, for the possibilities were limited, and the quest for pasturage, water, and fuel was unceasing. Usually the women and young children walked behind a wagon picking up buffalo and cow chips to throw into a canvas suspended under the wagon. At times, along some creek or other there were twigs, broken branches, and bark to be found.

The plain was gently rolling, but the travelers were scarcely aware of occasional slopes until the oxen leaned into their yokes and the long whips cracked, urging them on. The children were, more often than not, hollow-eyed and tired. The excitement of the start waned, and the days became for them endlessly monotonous. Usually they rode in the wagons packed with food and gear, but when the hills were steep or the slopes before them long they walked to ease the load on the oxen.

Above them was the vast dome of the sky, an enormous sky, stretching from horizon to horizon, all about them. No doubt the sky had always been like that, but back home it had always been broken by trees, an old barn, a church steeple, or a hill. Now there was nothing but a hollow distance and wind moving the grass.

There were no clouds. The men gathered together, talking in low tones so as not to alarm the women. But the women knew.

There was no water.

The barrels tied to the sides of the wagons sloshed when they moved, warning of how little was left. Last night they had made dry camp where water had been expected. The mud in the water hole was cracked and dried. What if the next one was dry, too?

When you had sixty wagons there would be six to eight yoke of oxen for each, there would be the few milk cows and riding horses along, and more than two hundred people. So you did not just need water; you needed a lot of water.

The boys who were ten, eleven, or older were out driving the cattle and any spare horses there were. Most of them carried rifles and would use them, for it was the horses and the cattle the Indians wanted. The cattle they wanted for eating—five or six Indians would eat a steer at one sitting. A boy of thirteen was expected to conduct himself like a man, and he did. He was still a boy, but he wanted to walk with the men and talk with the men and be respected for the work he did.

The wagons were not just anything with wheels. Back at Westport or Independence, in Missouri, the wagon master and several others inspected each wagon before it was permitted to join the train. The wagon had to be strongly made and the stock in good shape. There was one ramshackle wagon in this lot, but the wagon master had made an exception. The wagon might be in bad shape, but the five young men with rifles that came with it were not. He looked at those cool-eyed young men from the mountains and knew their presence was worth whatever trouble the wagon might cause.

That was what the wagon master was there for. To make judgments. Usually he had been over the trail before. He knew the problems and had learned to measure the people against his experience.

There were always a few who would turn back. They had listened and talked and had been carried along by the enthusiasm of others, but when the vast plains began to stretch out before them they quailed, beaten before they started. All of them were a little afraid. After all, they were leaving behind all they knew and much they loved, and they were going into a new world with its trials, dangers, and troubles, far from home and the familiar.

Yet they learned to cope. There was no one on whom to lean. A man on the frontier must make his own decisions and act upon them. Consequently, there was no subservience. Those who solve problems for themselves become confident. They trust to their own abilities.

So it was on the way west. Every day on the moving wagons brought problems, and every day they were solved and the wagons rolled on. Yet another change was taking place, and it was a fundamental one. Back at home when a man had problems he went to the minister or priest, to a banker or judge for advice. On the frontier he learned to go to the handyman, the man who could fix a broken wheel, fit an iron tire to a wagon, or repair a broken gun. He often discovered that the handyman was also able to offer practical, homely advice in other areas. Speculations on the Holy Trinity or the ideal world were for leisure time around a campfire. What the pioneer wanted to know was what do I do *now*?

One estimate has it that seventeen people died for every westward mile of the covered wagons. I think the estimate is a modest one. So many died of whom there is no record. Years later the remains of wagons might be found, merely a few scattered bones and nothing to identify anyone. In one case, Captain Eugene Ware when on patrol up

Lodgepole Creek found sixteen wagons, all neatly circled, grass grown up around them, some weathered harness, wagons showing every evidence of having been where they were for years. There was no food or ammunition left and the trunks had been ripped open and hastily looted. No letters, papers, or any marks of identification could be found. Although the story was widely reported at the time, nothing ever came of it, and the wagons remain a mystery, their owners vanished and unknown.

One group started with sixteen men and thirty-five mules, and one hundred thirty days later in California, broke and in rags, there were but ten men left and twenty-four mules.

As the move to the west increased with the advent of the so-called Gold Rush, wagon trains were banded together with less care; hence troubles increased and breakdowns became more frequent. The breaking of wheels was not uncommon, and shrinkage due to dryness of the air was to be expected. As a result, iron tires often fell off and had to be replaced. Spokes loosened in their sockets, and often men worked through the night to prepare their wagon for a start at daylight.

After the wind there was the rain, driving rainstorms that turned creeks into raging rivers where crossing was impossible until the rivers returned to normal. Even then the banks would be deep in mud, and it often required three teams to each wagon to move them across. That was when the small sheet-iron stoves carried in the wagons proved their value, for the fuel was wet and soggy and the weather impossible, but in the wagons coffee could be made and some comforting amount of food, though far shy of a good meal.

There were not always other wagon trains in close proximity. As the season stretched out and the time for crossing the Sierras grew close, the lines thinned out and the faces of the men grew taut with worry. Even before the Donner party, others had been trapped in the snows, and all knew the danger.

Actual attacks on wagon trains by Indians were few, but they did happen. More often, Indians simply drove off cattle and horses or struck any wagon that fell behind. Sir Francis Drake is a hero for his attacks on Spanish treasure galleons, but to the Indian a covered wagon was just as enticing a target.

The case of Fanny Kelly is an illustration. Her husband had, at her pleading, made every effort to conciliate the Indians, giving them food and other presents. Nevertheless, they attacked the train, killed several

people, and carried off Fanny and her sister's child. Later, when still not too far from the line of travel, Fanny Kelly managed to slip Mary down from her horse, having whispered to her what she must do to get back to the wagons. Later the child was found by Indians, shot with arrows, and scalped.

Such stories were told at every encampment and most wagon trains were well guarded, yet any small train or lone wagon was in great trouble.

Twelve miles was a good day's travel. With horses or mules that distance could be increased to twenty to twenty-five miles, but there are many records of wagon trains having traveled but three or four miles in a day, or even camping within sight of the previous day's camp.

Much depended on the nature of the terrain. A steep hill might require hours to negotiate and the hitching of several teams to each wagon. After heavy rains the plains were a sea of mud, and the heavy wagons could move but slowly. As they traveled further west and their food supplies were gradually reduced, the wagons grew lighter. Ahead of them waited the desert.

Most of them soon learned how to handle each situation. At first they had to invent, but then invention became an established procedure handled with speed and efficiency. For instance, where there was a danger of quicksand they learned to water the horses before crossing a stream so they would not stop for a drink and let their feet sink into the sand, from which it might be very difficult to extricate them.

Not all the wagons carried settlers moving west; many carried freight or supplies bound for the forts along the way or for sale in California or Oregon. The only other way for goods to reach the west coast was by ship around Cape Horn or by transport across the Isthmus of Panama.

In 1865, 6,000 wagons passed Fort Kearney in five weeks, and it is estimated that 22 million tons of freight were transported west in that year.

The crossing of the Continental Divide near South Pass came in the midst of an open plain after a long, steady climb, and the descent on the western slope was equally undramatic, but the worst of the travel lay ahead. The grass was scarcer, the water holes further apart. Crossing the deserts of the Great Basin and the passes of the Sierras presented a terrible ordeal that called for all the judgment and skill acquired on the long trek westward.

Whatever was left that could be discarded was thrown out to lighten the wagons for the oxen, mules, or horses, worn by day after day of marching. At Ragtown, as it was called, in Nevada, were acres of discarded books, chairs, dressers, dishes, and keepsakes, many of which had come from Europe with the first pioneers. Many a woman looked back at the few precious things brought from home that lay abandoned there. Only one thought remained, to get through, to get to California or Oregon, whichever was the destination, to find gold or a home.

By now they were veterans of the trail, and once at its end their trials would only begin, for to travel is one thing, to arrive at a destination something else. Here there were new problems, and the wagon train broke up, each traveler to go his or her own way. Wagons had been abandoned by some, men and women had died, some had found new mates, children had been born. Plans made in Ohio, Illinois, or Missouri were somehow less realistic at the journey's end.

Of those who returned east, some were disappointed, others had achieved their goals. All were richer for their experience. Many remained to build, to create, to establish themselves in the new land. They had learned how to pioneer, when to adjust. They had discovered that the ability to adapt was the ability to survive. They were made stronger by the knowledge that they could do what had to be done.

pages 86-87: Live oaks in Santa Ynez Range, California.

THE MISSISSIPPI

They heard about it long before they saw it, that great river in the west. First they heard from the Indians, and then from the Long Hunters. "A mile wide," some said, "a mile of rushing brown water carrying great, uprooted trees. And there's floating islands. Nobody knows where all that water comes from." Others scoffed. "It's a few hundred yards wide, that's all, but it is a big river."

The Father of Waters, the Indians called it, and there was no other river like it. The waters of the Ohio were lost in it, and there was another river, farther west, a great muddy river that added its stream, discoloring the water for miles.

It was a time for legend, a time of willing belief. Too many fantastic things had already happened to the westward bound, and their imaginations were prepared to accept what they were told.

They had access to no such information as we have today; those who might have read of De Soto's discovery were few indeed, and scarcely more had heard of Marquette or La Salle. Their only information came from Indians or chance travelers, who might know no more than they themselves. Maybe a long hunter squatted beside their campfire and spoke of the great river and its tributaries.

They dreamed of cities beside the river, of ships sailing up from the sea; at the very least, they dreamed of barges down the river to New Orleans. They knew of Louisiana: surely it was a market for furs, for logs, for whatever they might grow or discover.

In the east, men were selling dreams. They even had maps of town sites and pictures of fabulous cities all laid out and waiting to be occupied. All that the towns needed, they said, was people. The would-be settlers listened to lectures on farming, logging, and trapping, and it all seemed so easy and ready just for the taking. Some bought lots, others farms, and others the houses pointed out in illustrations. They sold what they had, gave up their jobs, gathered such equipment as they were told they would need, and went west.

In vain, steamboat captains told them there were no such places. Some believed the captain a liar, some that he wanted it all for himself. The salesmen had sold well, and dreams are the easiest things to sell.

Rollingstone was such a place: when they arrived, there was only a low-lying plain beside the river—no ready-built houses, no pleasantly curving lanes. They had been robbed and betrayed, but they would not relinquish the dream. Some went ashore and built sod houses or bought rafted planks. Winter came, cold and unforgiving. Few had enough fuel, and many died. Finally they gave up and departed, the few who survived the winter. They left to pursue other, easier dreams, elsewhere.

From the first the Mississippi and its tributaries the Ohio, Missouri, and Arkansas offered easy access, opening the country to exploration, settlement, and commerce. Yet these were attained only at great risk, for each of the streams offered its own traps for the unwary; navigating the Mississippi and the Missouri was particularly chancy. The channels were constantly changing, and great trees, torn from the banks, often had their roots buried in the silt of the river bottom, leaving the top of the tree to bob in the stream, sometimes only barely visible. The

page 90: Mississippi River, Perrot State Park, Wisconsin.
page 91: Bald cypress and knees; Reelfoot Lake, Tennessee.
page 93: Mississippi River, Pikes Peak State Park, Iowa.

planters, or sawyers, as they were called, could rip the bottom from the largest of boats, and often did so.

A pilot on either the Mississippi or the Missouri had to be ready for anything, and most of them were. Yet none was prepared for the events of December 1811 or the months that followed.

The most devastating earthquake ever to occur in North America within historical times struck near New Madrid, Missouri, at that time. The shocks were felt over an area many times greater than that of the better-known San Francisco earthquake and were felt as far as Savannah, Georgia; Charleston, South Carolina; and Richmond, Virginia. Severe shocks were felt over an area of a million square miles.

Great bluffs along the Mississippi and the Ohio tumbled into the rivers, trees two to three feet thick were snapped off like toothpicks, and the bed of the Mississippi itself was tilted so that the river flowed upstream. Several villages were destroyed, including New Madrid itself, and Reelfoot Lake, in Tennessee, was created when the surface of the land fell eight feet, causing the river waters to rush in and fill the basin just created.

Several eyewitnesses have left accounts of the quake as they experienced it; the best account is probably that of John Bradbury, as told in his *Travels in the Interior of America*. Bradbury was a naturalist and an experienced observer of natural phenomena.

The quake occurred at 2 A.M., and by daylight there had been twenty-seven shocks of varying strength. The town of New Madrid, which seems to have been at the epicenter or close to it, dropped approximately eight feet. Houses were thrown down, whole forests of trees toppled, and spouts of water shot up through cracks in the earth.

The area now covered by Reelfoot Lake had been thick forest, and some trees remain, growing in the water. The lake is on the flyway of migrating birds; more than 250 varieties have been seen there. Reelfoot River and Bayou de Chien drain into the lake and help to maintain its water level. The lake is eighteen miles long and in some places up to three miles wide.

Life along the great river has always been extraordinary but never so much as in pioneer days. Settlements were springing up along the river, some to last for many years, some to die within months, but all were subject to traffic on the river and looked to it for supplies, for craftsmen, and for entertainment.

Flatboats were often floating museums or traveling shows, and more often than not there were floating churches, if one wished to call them so. An evangelist, usually accompanied by at least one singer, more often by a troupe, would visit each town along the river trying to save sinners, most of whom were willing to be saved for the excitement of it. Often enough the "saving" lasted, but just as often the sinner backslid once the floating revival meeting had passed on along the river.

There were floating stores, bringing supplies to the settlers. They brought food, of course, but also dress goods and leather boots, saddles, and harness. Some carried blacksmiths or coopers, ready to shoe a horse, repair a gun, or make a plow or a barrel. And all this went on before the steamboats came to enliven the rivers still more.

Docks as such rarely existed; usually a boat just nosed into the bank and let down a gangway to load and unload passengers or freight.

The river merchants were buying as well as selling; often they provided the only market the remote river villages had except for such far-off places as New Orleans, Natchez, and St. Louis. Trappers brought their furs to be swapped or sold. Cash money was hard to come by along the river, but every pioneer was a trader and relished the trading. A skillful trader could become a rich man, and many were the tales of men who started out with nothing but a few furs and a wagonload or boatload of apples and returned after weeks with everything that could be imagined. Trading seemed to come naturally to the people from the hills or along the rivers. It was not only business, it was pleasure, and often more fun than a poker game or a rough-and-tumble fight. And the riverboats then and later were noted for their fighting men.

The steamboat pilots, when their time came, were the aristocracy of the river, looked up to by all and admired by small boys who wished only to grow up to become pilots themselves. It was somewhat the same with stage drivers further west and east.

The river, whether at the time of the steamboats or before, was pure romance. Rough and hard, yes, but a colorful, moving panorama of excitement.

Old-timers along the river all said there was no sound anywhere like the sound of a steamboat whistle, as a ship came in for a landing. It was the same as the long, lonely whistle of the old steam trains in later years, or the deep-throated blast of an oceangoing ship headed for the sea. So many sounds cling to the memory, and often it needs only such a sound to bring back a flood of memories, of forgotten voices and forgotten faces.

The river was a place for happenings, a place for memories. People lived near it, on it, and with it, yet they feared it even as they loved it, for the river had the power to rise and destroy. Every old-timer had stories of floods and of wrecked boats or of steamboat races, explosions, and in the old days, river pirates.

To most of those going west it was only a river to be crossed, the first of many. Only when they had put the Mississippi behind them could they set out across the Great Plains, only then could they follow their dreams.

Yet to those who lived along the river, the river was enough; they wanted no more, they needed no more.

I N D I A N S

There are as many Indians living in the United States and Canada today as when Columbus first came to America. Moreover, in proportion to their numbers as many Indians have succeeded in our society as any other ethnic group. As most of these successful Indians have Anglo names, they are often not recognized as such when their names appear on boards of directors or in the public press.

The life-styles of the Indians were dictated to a great extent by the area in which they lived, but by and large theirs was a hunting-and-gathering economy, although some were successful planters and relied to an extent on the produce of their fields.

Their lodges varied according to their life-style and the land in which they lived, from the longhouses of the Iroquois to the earth lodges of the Mandans, the buffalo-hide tipi of the Plains Indian, and the stone or adobe houses of the southwest. Although there were threads that ran through language groups, there were divergences, too.

97

To use the term "Indian" is to oversimplify. The Indians adapted themselves and their way of life to the country about them. They suffered from lack of contact with outside cultures that might have prompted change. Europe, with its many rivers and harbors, as well as waves of migrating peoples, benefited from these spurs to creativity and change.

Indians created a warring society, and among most Indian peoples the only way to attain status was by taking scalps or counting coups. In its purest form counting coups meant striking a living, armed enemy and getting away. Later, as with customs in all cultures, the meaning was broadened to include the striking of any enemy, living or dead, which accounts for the dozens of arrows found shot into the bodies of the dead.

It has been frequently stated, and repeated by authors who should know better, that the scalping of enemies was introduced by the white man. This is simply not true, and the evidence is all to the contrary.

This idea undoubtedly had its origin in the fact that during the French and Indian War, which began in 1754, both the French and the English paid bounties for scalps. This practice persisted in the various wars and troubles that followed, but the scalping of enemies was an ancient custom, as an abundance of testimony proves.

Garcilaso de la Vega in his work *The Florida of the Inca* tells of scalping, and Charles Hudson in his excellent work *The Southeastern Indians* speaks of this and adds, "Scalping was evidently an old practice in the south-east. The first Europeans to encounter it were De Soto's soldiers who saw it inflicted on fallen comrades as they entered Apalachee territory in northern Florida. They observed that the Apalachees sometimes tied scalps to their bows as decorations.

"We have at least some prehistorical evidence of scalping. At Moundville, for example, the skull of a young woman was found to have a shallow groove at approximately the hair-line which ran horizontally around the skull. She was probably scalped and survived to suffer an infection at the line where the incision was made."

Marc Lescarbot, in his *Nova Francia,* published in 1606, tells of scalping. Cartier visited Hochelaga in the winter of 1535–36 and commented that the Indians had a habit of decorating walls with scalps.

John Lawson, surveyor general of Carolina told of scalping in his fine work *A New Voyage to Carolina.* Lawson was a naturalist of sorts and wrote one of the first books on the area. Ironically, he was later tortured, killed, and scalped himself. His book was published in 1709.

John Brickell, M.D., in his *The Natural History of North Carolina*, published in Dublin in 1737, also speaks of scalping. He spent much time in the Carolinas.

William Byrd, in his *History of the Dividing Line Betwixt Virginia and North Carolina*, published in 1728, also tells of scalping. Byrd's book was written while surveying the line of which he speaks and in the weeks following his return.

Champlain tells of scalping as a practice among the Indians, in 1603.

Most of the explorers in all parts of the continent had comments to make on scalping, including Jean Bernard Bossu and Gaspar José de Solis. The latter told of the practice in his *Diary of a Visit of Inspection to the Texas Mission*. Pierre Radisson, who had himself been tortured by Indians, discussed the practice.

At various places and times the practice differed in its method as well as in the reasons for it. Some tribes did not scalp at all, but that the custom was an ancient one is indicated by recent discoveries at a dig near Crow Creek, South Dakota, where there is evidence of scalping during a massacre sometime after 1200 A.D.

The scalp was considered a symbol of victory over an enemy as well as an example of a warrior's prowess in battle, yet among some tribes only one scalp needed to be taken for use in the elaborate ceremonies that followed. The scalp was used in such cases to pacify the spirits of enemies killed in battle.

A similar custom persists among us in the symbols painted on the sides of fighter planes and tanks representing enemy planes downed, ships sunk, or tanks destroyed.

above: Petroglyphs; Newspaper Rock, Canyonlands, Utah.
page 101: Shoshone Cove, on Horse Prairie Creek, Montana.

THE BIG BEND

It's big country and it is rough country, lying in the big Texas bend of the Rio Grande with Mexico on the other side of the river. It was Apache country once and bandit country later. Rustlers operated on both sides of the border, stealing cattle in the United States to be sold in Mexico and stealing cattle in Mexico to be sold in the United States.

The Apache, of course, recognized no borders. He rode over the land as an eagle flies over it, ignoring the white man's rules and regulations. Until the coming of the white man the only enemies to be faced were the Comanches, and one of the favored Comanche raiding routes led right through the Big Bend.

The two peoples waged many a bitter fight. One of the most famous occurred when Bajo El Sol challenged the right of the Apache to pass through the country. Bajo El Sol was slain in the resulting battle, but not until he had made a name long remembered among the peoples of both tribes.

page 102: Rio Grande River, Texas-Mexico border.
page 103: Rio Grande River, near Langtry, Texas.
above: Sunrise mists; Chisos Mountains, Big Bend National Park, Texas.

One branch of the Comanche Trail crossed the Rio Grande near Boquillas and another at Presidio, joining at Comanche Springs to cross the country to Yellow Horse Draw, where Lubbock now stands. The trail had many meanderings, and although the main trail was generally followed the Comanche often deviated to go by other routes because of enemies or changing water conditions.

The Big Bend offers a parade of those wonderful American names that Stephen Vincent Benét wrote of in his poem that ends with the line "bury my heart at Wounded Knee."

Persimmon Gap, Shot Tower Peak, Lost Mine Peak, Panther Springs Draw, Elephant Tusk, the Chisos Mountains, Terlingua, Burro Mesa, Dogie Mountains, Mariscal Canyon, Packsaddle and Hen Egg Mountains, Slickrock, Paint Gap Hills, Smuggler's Gap, Hell's Half Acre, Mule Ear, Nine Point, and Study Butte.

It is a land of stark beauty, and in the light of the changing day it seems never twice the same. The sunlight and shadow on the mountainsides deepen the canyons and crest the ridges with gold and rose. It is a fantastic land more akin to parts of Arizona and Nevada than to Texas, yet not the same. The Big Bend has an aura and a mystique of its own.

Texas Rangers knew every corner of it, as did such bandits as Chico Cano, Gacho, and others too numerous to name. Cano's two brothers, Manuel and José, were as feared as he was. There were many killings, as well as raids upon lonely ranches and stores. For years the Big Bend was a frontier of its own, and in some respects it still is.

A large part of the Big Bend is now a national park, comprising some 788,682 acres. A silver mine was worked at Boquillas, Mexico, just over the border, and the quicksilver mines at Terlingua were widely known.

There were three aspects to life in the Big Bend. The Mexicans, the Anglo-Americans, and the smugglers. The last named rarely lived in the Big Bend country, but they passed through, using old Indian trails or making trails of their own. Some were Mexicans, some were Anglos, but by and large they were not appreciated by the inhabitants.

It is an arid land, but wild, beautiful, and picturesque. There are ruined villages, deserted ranches, the remains of old campfires. Cottonwoods grow along the river, and the higher mountains are timbered with fir or piñon pine. Smoking beside their doorways, the old Mexicans have many stories to tell. There are mysterious travelers in the night and ghost lights in the mountains. The young men look at them and wonder, while the old people cross themselves and turn away.

Any road leading south from Marfa, Alpine, or Marathon will take you into the Big Bend country, but it is not a place to simply go, look, and return. To really feel the Big Bend one must take time, loiter a bit, eat in the villages or at a ranch home, and get the feel of the country itself. The people are quiet, minding their own affairs but missing nothing of what goes on about them. They are a gentle people, but it is always wise to remember that many of them have Apache blood, and when you hear a whispering in the night and something stirs the leaves in passing, who is to say it is not Alsate or Bajo El Sol leading a ghostly war party along the trails of memory?

below: Agave shoot and Casa Grande rock, Big Bend National Park, Texas.
page 107: Rio Grande River and Santa Elena Canyon, Big Bend National Park, Texas.

G H O S T T O W N S

They belong to the desert now, or the high mountain ranges. They have given themselves to the earth. Grass grows in the old corrals, roof shingles have curled under the sun, and when winter winds blow down the pass elk sometimes take shelter in the saloon where bearded miners drank, swore, and told tall tales. A table that knew the whisper of cards and the rattle of poker chips is tipped on its side, one leg broken. A few scattered chips and faded cards still lie about.

The mountainside, once stripped of trees to build cabins or to timber mines, is growing into forest again. A marmot has taken up residence under the floor of the assay office, and there's a broken pick lying on the dump at the mine called Rainbow's End.

A sentinel chimney marks where the blacksmith shop stood, and there's a stretch of boardwalk, gray and splintered, across the street from the saloon. There are no buildings beside the walk, only three foundations, their materials long since taken away to build elsewhere or burned in campfires. One was a saloon, and the faded sign lies there proclaiming The Glory Hole, amid a few smoke-blackened bricks.

All things change in the mountains. Sand becomes sandstone and then quartzite; gravel becomes conglomerate and then gneiss; mud changes to shale, to slate, and then to schist; shells change to limestone and then to marble. Nothing remains the same as the years become centuries and the centuries, millenniums.

The houses where men lived fall and feed their richness back into the earth to grow new grass and new trees, and in those years the deer, elk, and bear will have it to themselves. The marmot now sitting in the door of the assay office will be followed by generations of marmots who will sun themselves on a small mound where that door once was.

Wind will blow down the pass, snow will fall and drift where the town once stood, and the memories of the town will fade from the memories of a few old men. The shouts and laughter that once sounded here will be heard only by lingering ghosts, and on the low hill outside of town the last gravemarker will fall and nobody will remember Two-Gun Jack or why he taunted the man at the end of the bar who simply shot him and walked away before Jack could tell him who he was. Which was grossly unfair as Two-Gun liked to tell people how dangerous he was before he shot them.

The sides of the mountain are dotted with old prospect holes where dreams of riches died before the reality of brutally hard work.

Ghost towns are where you find them; most are in the west but certainly not all. Most were in mining country where an ore discovery brought men flocking to open mines, to sell goods, entertainment, or supplies, and from where they disappeared just as quickly when the mines played out or too much water flowed in.

Usually, a few held on. They had faith. Their town would come back. There was a lot of ore down there yet, they said. All they needed was to pump out the water that flooded the diggings. Landslides and

page 108: End of the line; Lake Valley—National Rail Line Remnant at Nutt, New Mexico.
page 109: Relic of Chinese restaurant; Gleason, Arizona.

fire dealt with some towns, but the greatest slayer of towns was lack of faith.

Many were in the desert; often they were in the very high mountain country covered every year by several feet of snow. Most of them are known to have had their brief moments in the sun, yet every so often one finds a town with no history, a town that was born and died so quickly that it left no mark. Its only record might be in the shipping addresses of some faraway manufacturer or supplier who sent them goods or tools. Some towns were born, lived fast, and died without a whimper.

Others that might have become ghost towns were kept alive by interested citizens who refused to let the town die, helped by an influx who traded on the reputation of bygone years. Books were written about them, and stories repeated; sometimes films were made and tourists came to visit. A few miners lingered on, working small claims or leasing from the larger mines. These towns often had names like Deadwood, Tombstone, Tonopah, Goldfield, and Cripple Creek.

The men and women who made them are gone, and we will not see their like again. Perhaps those who followed were just as brave, strong, and enduring, but they were different, the old ones who fol-

Adobe along Jemez River, New Mexico.

lowed the booms, going from camp to camp to be where the money was, and the excitement, and their old companions.

Bat Masterson, Wyatt Earp and his brothers, Mysterious Dave Mather, Langford Peel, Jim Levy, John Bull, Doc Holliday, and dozens of others. The ones written about were the flashy, the notorious. Then there were the others, the women who worked on the line or in the dance halls, the stage drivers, the saloon keepers, and, of course, the merchants and suppliers.

Wherever a mining camp boomed, they came on the run. If they were not the first comers they arrived shortly after. The professional peace officers arrived, too, and were often hired. They knew the crowd, who was who and how to handle them. Some you could talk to, some needed taming, others you could awe, but there were always a few who would need the attention of the local uplift society—who did their lifting with a rope.

Often the road they traveled is abandoned. The grass does cosmetic service to the ruts they left, and the scattered cans grow thin and brown. The harsh glare of bottles lying in the sun is muted to softer blue or lavender as the sunlight does its work upon the glass.

The old towns, the ghost towns, no longer belong to men. The desert and the mountains have taken them back, gathered them into their arms and made them one with the trees and brush and rocks. The old tunnels are caves where animals live, and the dreams that gave them birth have died or been carried on to other places.

I like to think the last is true, for does a dream ever die? Does it not live on, aching to be realized? If not by you, by someone.

page 112: *Relics of the past; Tincup, Colorado.*
above: *Tailings and buildings; Red Mountain, San Juan Range, Colorado.*

THE WIND RIVER RANGE

Two of my books, *Bendigo Shafter* and *Under the Sweetwater Rim*, have dealt with this area. The first gold is reported to have been discovered here in 1842, but the Indians proved less than friendly so nothing was done about it until much later. There is evidence of some work in 1860, but not until 1867 did the town boom. Within a few months the population was over 4,000 people, and neighboring towns such as Atlantic City (so called because it was on the east side of the Continental Divide) and Miner's Delight caught some of the overflow.

The wind came cold off the Wind River Range, and miners were ever a fickle lot. If gold did not show in sufficient quantities they swung their packs to their backs and hit the trail to look for better ground. South Pass City was born, boomed briefly, and died, but in the interval there were enough differences of opinion to build a fair-sized Boot Hill where some rather abrupt citizens arrived after coming to a very abrupt end.

It was the custom of the time to carry pistols, and they were often referred to when disputes arose. When Judge Colt rendered a verdict the case was rarely appealed, which caused lawyers to hasten the arrival of law and order before they starved to death.

Remarkable for few things, South Pass City had a lady resident, a young widow named Esther Hobart Morris, who held a tea party for two rival candidates and prevailed upon whoever won to move for women's suffrage. William H. Bright, who won, introduced the bill that brought Wyoming into the Union as the first state allowing women the vote. Esther Hobart Morris then became the first woman ever elected to public office in the United States. She became justice of the peace in 1870. In the east the question was still to be debated for years, but in the west nobody had any doubt of women's equality and voted their convictions.

As for Boot Hill, Mountain Jack Alvarese, Vinegar Zeriner, and a couple of dozen others added their remains to the Wyoming soil, all losers in pistol arbitrations. Occasional Indian raids added others to local safe-deposit areas, for the Cheyenne, Sioux, and Arapahoe paid quick visits to the area when no other amusements were available.

By the time they had burned the stage stations and chased the stagecoaches and pony express riders, the miners working their claims were all that remained of South Pass City. All this activity provided blood and thunder for conversations over the bars of South Pass City's thirteen saloons, and no doubt more Indians were killed over the bars of South Pass City than ever existed west of the Mississippi.

The town had its other problems. Among its hotels was one where rumor claimed that more customers went in than ever came out. If they did come out it was at night, to be buried in the yard or under the stable.

The gold the miners found did not last long, and fortune seekers began to drift away. A few remained to work for day wages, nursing the hope, as some always did, that the town would come back. To the north lay the Wind River and the Wind River Valley, where Major Noyes

page 114: Atlantic City, Wyoming.
page 115: Badlands; South Pass and Wind River, Wyoming.
page 117: Crazy Creek Cascade, Beartooth Mountains, Wyoming-Montana border.

Baldwin settled and opened a trading establishment. Baldwin had led a group of forty men in exploring the South Pass area in 1865 and had gone up the Valley to Wind River. Chief Washakie of the Shoshones was friendly, as the Shoshones under him always had been (they fought beside the Army in battles with the Sioux) and welcomed the settlers.

It was a striking, picturesque country, far more pleasant than the vicinity of South Pass.

Old Indian trails wind among the high peaks above timberline, and there are places one can see where the Indians built or repaired ancient trails. There are high, lonely lakes, snowfields, even glaciers. Wyoming has many beautiful mountain ranges, the Big Horns, Wind Rivers, Tetons, Absarokas, and others. Although the Tetons are perhaps the best known I confess a preference for the Wind River and Absaroka ranges. This is a purely personal preference with which I ask no one to agree.

It is a uniquely beautiful country and I envy only the men who saw it first.

Island Lake and peaks of the Bridger Wilderness, Wind River Range, Wyoming.

H I D E O U T S

There are places I've been of which I shall not tell, lonely places, better left alone. There are hideouts in the hills where no man ever hid, lying there waiting to be needed. Often, in such places, I have built my campfires, taking care to keep the fire small and to use just what fuel was lying about. If someone has been before me I build my fire where he built his, to trespass no more than I must.

Occasionally I have walked where bears walk, or deer, and have sat under the aspen and watched beaver at work. I am never surprised when people claim to have seen the Loch Ness monster or the *yeti* and have no pictures. The best sightings of wild animals I have had were when I was without a camera or in some cases could not get it into action in time.

Once, walking up an old Indian trail in the Santa Rosas of southern California, I came to the end of a sugar loaf of hill and found myself,face-to-face with a magnificent bighorn. We were no more than a dozen feet apart and mutually astonished. I had a Rollei suspended around my neck by its strap and very carefully I lifted my hands to get the picture, but as the top snapped into place the ram ducked into the canyon and when I saw him again he was almost perfectly camouflaged by cactus, rock, and brush on the next hillside.

Often I hike the mountains and desert, but when alone I do more loitering than hiking. When one adopts a goal that is miles away one misses too much. If one is to understand and appreciate the wilderness one should stroll along, pause, sit down for a while and just absorb what there is to see, to hear, to smell. Walking too fast one misses too much. If you see a wild animal at such a time it is strictly by accident. If you sit quietly and make no sound they often appear. I have had deer come to feed within fifty feet of me when I was downwind of them.

The mere fact that you do not see animals does not mean they are not present. Usually they see you first and quietly disappear into the landscape. From time to time a would-be explorer goes into the jungle or mountains searching for some strange animal of which he has heard. A few weeks later he returns saying there is no such beast because he found none. I have spent years in mountains where there were mountain lions, yet the only two I have seen were treed by dogs; that was in the Tonto Basin country.

I have seen their tracks, and upon one occasion in Colorado one obviously followed me for some distance. There was a saddle in the hill over which I'd never crossed, and wishing to see what lay on the other side I walked a sandy old cow trail to the crest of the saddle. For several minutes I stood there looking across a lovely green meadow at the aspen. Returning I found a lion track superimposed on mine. No doubt he had followed a hunter at some time and eaten what the hunter left. No doubt he hoped to do the same with whatever I killed, only I was not hunting.

There was, in Arizona, a high, comblike ridge of dark red rock that loomed above what was then the highway. At its base there was a

---

page 120: Sandstone forms; Valley of Fire State Park, Nevada.
page 121: Valley of Fire State Park, Nevada.

black hole, apparently a cave. For months I drove by en route to the mine where I was employed at the time, always telling myself that some day I would climb up and have a look.

Years passed, and one day when again in the area, I pulled off to the side of the road and leaving my friends waiting, climbed the steep talus slope. The ridge was, as things always are in the west, farther away than it appeared, and when I reached the base of the ridge that small dark hole was all of thirty feet high and half as broad, and not at all interesting. It was not a cave, merely a sort of alcove in the rock wall.

Walking along the base of the wall, I discovered something not visible from below. The wall was broken and overlapped at one point. Walking into the cleft I found a narrow opening on my left, an opening thickly packed with thorny shrub making passage extremely difficult. Beyond I could see green grass and the leaves of a cottonwood tree. There was an open space of perhaps an acre, and the cottonwoods and color of the grass were indications of water.

It was late afternoon and we had far to go. My friends were waiting, so I explored no further. Perhaps what I saw was all there was, but it is or could be the perfect hideout. I have not been back.

A man traveling wild country in the old days always kept his eyes open for possible camping places, not only for the immediate journey but for some future time. Those things essential for a camp—shelter from the wind, fuel, and water—were the same essentials for the Indian or for prehistoric man, and often on the sites chosen I have found evidence of previous use, sometimes from the pioneer years or earlier.

Unfortunately, much of the knowledge of terrain acquired by mountain men in the course of their hunting and trapping was never written down, for the simple reason that it seemed too obvious. By simple observation they learned to read the land, to tell directions by plant growth or by melting snow, and to find the easiest routes of travel.

Buffalo and other wild game had found the best trails long before any white man and probably before any Indian. Engineers who came to lay out roads or railroads usually found they could not improve on buffalo trails, which always followed the easiest way.

In traveling wild country it is always best to stay with the trail, for a trail is always going somewhere and is usually the shortest route

between points. Whenever I have left a trail, except for a bit of exploration, I have gotten into trouble. Once, following a long, wind-about trail I came upon a long, beautiful slope of grass leading down to the very point where I wished to go. A car waited for me down there, and the trail led off in a roundabout way, so I decided on the shortcut. I was tired. It had been a long day, and the easy way down the grassy slope was inviting. After nearly two miles I came suddenly to a deep canyon, dropping sheer for three hundred feet, and no way down. Across the canyon that nice grassy slope continued, but I had to walk all the way back to the trail, and it was all uphill. Common sense should have told me that had there been an easy way down others would have used it.

Nobody *knows* the wild country. No matter how long one lives in it and with it one is forever learning, and there is always much to see and hear. Nor are any two places the same.

Much of what one gets from the wilderness depends on what one takes to it. By this I mean that the more that is known of simple geology, of plant growth, and so on, the more interesting an area becomes. The point is not only to see what is there but to know what is happening and what has happened. Soon one is able to travel the country with an awareness impossible before.

If you believe the wilderness is gone you are mistaken. It is out there, miles upon miles of it, but passersby must leave it as they found it, always remembering that it is the land from which we have come and that it is to the land we return in times of great trouble.

---

page 124: Cave Creek Canyon, Chiricahua Mountains, Arizona.
page 125: Paria River Canyon, Utah.

Natural Bridge, Alabama

IN THE NEVADA MOUNTAINS

We turned off the highway near the old Broken Toe mine on a dirt road that led into the Monte Cristo mountains of Nevada. There were no recent tire tracks.

We had driven out of Tonopah before daylight, and now the rising sun had turned the mountains to flame. Their color was a high pink at any time, but at dawn or sunset with the changing shadows and lights their colors were not to be believed.

"Pa was a mining man," the Judge said, "but he made enough to put me through college. He had faith in the Monte Cristos, so I've kept up the assessment work."

"Come back in five days," I told him. "I should be through by then."

"You'll be all right out here alone?"

"I've been alone most of my life, and when a man does assessment work on mining claims he must expect to be alone."

The road was no more than a trail with long stretches of deep dust and too bumpy for conversation. When he spoke again it was to

say, "I suppose I'm a fool. The only good strike Pa ever made was near Tonopah."

"I was in on the last gold rush in the country," I commented, "at Weepah."

He glanced at me. "That came to nothing."

"Nothing much."

We were climbing now. "There's water in the seeps not far from the claim. If that plays out, the nearest source I know of is nine or ten miles east near the old mill site." Water worried me. This was dry country.

The claim wasn't much to look at, but they rarely were. It was a hollow in the hills with a few juniper and some sagebrush. There was the beginning of a tunnel into the side of a low hill. It was no more than six feet into the mountain.

We unloaded the supplies, as well as a pick, a shovel, a single jack, and some drills. There was a box of giant powder and some fuses.

"You've got to be careful with that fuse," he said.

"I've used it."

He glanced around. "Well, I suppose I'd better get back to the office."

He hesitated, glanced at me again, and got into the car. He looked like he was going to say something but just put the car into gear and rolled off. At the turn when he left the claim for the road he waved. I lifted a hand in response.

For a few minutes I listened to the dwindling sound of the car and its jolting passage over the rough road, and then I was alone.

He was a lawyer who had been a minor judge of some kind. At least, they called him Judge. He looked about thirty-five and probably was closer to fifty, a quiet man, not really comfortable when out of the town.

There was a ring of stones where somebody had built a fire, but it was a sitting fire, and there was no good place near it to roll out a bed, so I found a flat spot, picked up a few rocks to make it better, and then moved the ring of stones to a better spot. I'd want the fire close to where I slept so I could stir it up in the morning. It was going to be cold up here at sunrise. The altitude was about six thousand feet and this was semidesert country, which chills rapidly when the sun goes down.

Nevada is a country of many small mountain ranges and a few big ones. It is an unfortunate thing that the most beautiful areas of some states lie far from the highways. Many people come to and go from Arizona for years and never see the magnificent mountains or pine forests in the east-central parts of the state or north of Flagstaff. In Nevada some of the prettiest areas are back in the mountains and far from towns.

Not far from where I sat on the rocks looking out over the country were many small ranges—the Toiyabe, the Toquema, Hot Creek, Monitor, San Antonio, and Cedar, to name a few. Some are bare, rugged mountains, some forested. In between lie long valleys—Big Smoky, Stone Cabin, Monitor, and others. It is a stark, rugged, wonderful country.

There was mineral in the country. Not far away were Coaldale and Sodaville, which were almost gone except for the shadows and a few people stirring around. They had found agate, chalcedony, and turquoise in the area, and, of course, some of the richest gold in the country had been found around Goldfield and Tonopah.

The Weepah rush that I'd mentioned came to nothing. I have never been back but believe there was one property that turned out rather well, for a time, at least. We came up from Arizona when we heard about the gold discovery, three of us with our bedrolls in an old jalopy.

We staked a claim on the outer edge of things where there was an outcropping that looked promising. Two days later I sold my share for fifty dollars, and as far as I know I was the only one of our group to pay expenses on the trip.

Two of our bunch stayed to work the claim, but the man who owned the jalopy and I drove back to Arizona and a job that paid wages and offered a boarding house.

A dozen times I'd driven past the Monte Cristos, always taking time out to admire their brilliant colors but driving on to somewhere else. Now for a few days I would be here, working in their midst.

The next morning I was up at daylight, denied myself the pleasure of scouting the country, and went to work. When other work had been hard to come by I'd often found that men owned claims in the mountains but were not eager to do the hard physical labor necessary to hold a claim. To file on a mining claim is one thing, to do the hundred dollars of work each year to hold it, quite another. To hire it done was not always easy, as most of those who could do it were looking for something more permanent. As for me, I was a drifter, interested in seeing the country, and for that purpose such jobs worked nicely for me.

As miners go, I couldn't qualify. Most of my time underground had been spent on the business end of a muckstick (shovel, to you) or tramming, which meant pushing an ore car that held either three-quarters of a ton or a ton of ore, depending on the car.

Assessment work such as I was now doing was usually nothing but labor to develop the property and bring it nearer to production. Few claims ever got so far, yet occasionally one was discovered that yielded some values and promised more. The wise prospector then sold quickly for the best price he could get. Bringing a mine into production is a costly project and unless the values are very good indeed may never repay the investment.

In the evenings after work I hiked along the mountain until I could get a good view over the Big Smoky Valley, and beyond it to the San Antonio Range and the Monitor, which was even higher. As the shadows grew longer the various ridges and hollows stood out, the latter in deep shadow, the former often crested with gold from the setting sun.

Fremont passed down the Big Smoky Valley in 1845, and Jedediah Smith crossed it higher up when he was bound for California. A wild and beautiful land then, it is so yet.

Drilling took most of my day, and in the late afternoon I would spit (light) the fuses and retire some distance to listen for the shots and count them. Counting the shots is important. If you load eight holes and only count seven shots, the next morning will demand great care. If the powder in a hole did not explode and you drill into it . . . !

Sometimes two shots will go off as one, but no chances can be taken.

For five days I drilled, blasted, and mucked out ore. In between times I worked to improve the road, digging out a few boulders and smoothing it down. It was hard work under a blazing sun, but the skies were clear and the air magnificent, and I had never minded hard work. Never much of a camp cook I usually ate from a can, made coffee cowboy style when the mood struck me, and read by the campfire.

In the five days I saw only one snake, a rattler who seemed disposed to get away from me, and I let it go. It was one of those pale rattlers scarcely to be seen against the sand if they lie still. Twice I saw mule deer, and tarantulas were common. It was a wise man who

page 128: Quartzite quarry and Wheeler Peak, Nevada.
page 129: Bristlecone pines; Snake Range, Nevada.
pages 130-131: Lupine and balsam root; Jarbidge Mountains, Nevada.
above: Granite forms; Newberry Mountains, Nevada.

Columbus Salt Flats, Nevada.

shook out his boots carefully in the morning before putting them on.

On the morning of the sixth day I was sitting beside the road with my tools gathered beside me, my pack ready, canteen filled at the seep, waiting. On the rocks nearby I had laid out a half dozen pieces of rock that looked promising.

The Judge's car could be heard long before he reached the claim. He looked at me as if to be sure I was all in one piece, then walked over to see what I had done. The tunnel into the hill was six feet deeper, the waste and ore mucked out, and the likely stuff (not very) stacked at one side.

"Have any trouble?"

"No."

We loaded the gear into the car and he noticed a book in my pack. "You read?"

"Every chance I get."

"See any wildlife?"

"Deer. They fed right close to camp."

"Weren't they frightened?"

"They looked at me, I looked at them, and they just kept on feeding."

He took the samples I'd saved. A couple of pieces looked pretty, and he would put them on a shelf in his office somewhere, just to look at.

"Must have been quiet," he said. "How can you stand being alone?"

"I wasn't alone," I said, "I had a mountain with me."

A couple of hours later when he had paid me and I was taking up my pack he said, "If you're around next year . . . ?"

"I won't be. I'll be sitting on another mountain, somewhere."

When I was a block down the street and nearing the highway, I looked back.

He was standing there, looking after me. He waved at me, and I waved back.

I never knew his name and he did not know mine. Not that it would have mattered.

THE SAN JUANS AND
THE LA PLATAS

If you look for Parrott City you will look in vain, nothing remains. It began in 1874 with a board laid across the tops of whiskey barrels to offer the first bar in town. It enjoyed a mild boom and was briefly the county seat. The town and a nearby mountain peak were named for Tiburcio Parrott, a San Francisco banker who grubstaked John Moss. It was Moss who located the site and laid out the town. He also named Starvation Creek.

In the summer of 1873 John Moss led a party of prospectors into the area to search for gold. Running short of supplies, Moss left several of the party encamped on a small mountain stream and rode off to New Mexico to equip for a longer stay. Shortly after, one of those who remained, Richard Giles, accidentally wounded himself, and the party were forced to remain where they were until the return of Moss.

His journey was long, and for those who remained it was a starving time. Some feared he had been killed by Indians, a needless

fear as John Moss spoke several Indian tongues and was well liked by Indians.

Moss did return, and the town of Parrott City was established. Later, when La Plata County was organized, Richard Giles became its first sheriff.

Parrott City was only one of several towns scattered along the canyon of the La Plata River, which flows down from Cumberland Basin. There is a winding road (you will need four-wheel drive) that follows the river up to the basin, which is at ten thousand feet and higher.

The road is rough and rocky, skirting the very edge of deep canyons, winding its narrow way through aspen groves, pines, and spruce to emerge at last in the basin. It is singularly beautiful, and when the season has been kind with rain or heavy snow, it is a flowering wonderland. Even in midsummer, snow will be found on the shady sides of the mountains or banked in the cirques formed by long-ago glaciers.

The skyline is rimmed with a magnificent line of peaks, many of them topping out at over twelve thousand feet, and a few reaching to fourteen. These are the San Juans, big brother to the La Platas and one of the most beautiful mountain ranges on earth.

Walk gently here, for this is tundra, and the plants are those you would find in the Arctic Circle. Their growing season is short, and plants destroyed take long to recover.

The air is thin, and one walks slowly, yet the air is clear and pure, scattered with white clouds, and on most afternoons there can be showers. The high mountains are no place to be in a thunderstorm, and I speak from experience.

Driving through Durango and on to Silverton and Ouray, one is continually in the San Juans with an amazing view of mountain and mountainside, of forest and plunging streams. It is truly an enormous country.

---

page 138: Top view, Uncompahgre Peak, San Juan Mountains, Colorado.
page 139: Columbine in Yankee Boy Basin, Colorado.
page 140: Autumn clearing in Dallas Divide; Sneffels Range, Colorado.

When first I came to this country I was nineteen, hunting a job in the mines. We rode the train from Durango to Silverton, but I had no luck finding a job, and on the return trip we got off at Needleton. My friend had a mining claim back in Vallecito Canyon and had to catch up on some assessment work, so I went along to lend a hand and to see the country. We hiked into Chicago Basin that first afternoon and camped for the night. There were some others working claims in the area or prospecting, I never did know which, and they stopped by to look us over and talk.

At daybreak we went over Columbine Pass and down into Vallecito. My friend's claim was above Johnson Creek, and I helped him for the first day, then hiked on up the canyon to Rock Creek and prowled around for a bit, getting back with the last rays of the sun. My friend wanted company more than help with the work, and there was too much to see. It was high mountain country and I was happy.

Another time I climbed to Hidden Lake and hiked in the country around Irving Peak. It was the first time I'd had any leisure since starting on my own, a result of saving my money and a lot of hard work, and this was country I loved. I wasn't in a hurry about anything at all, and now and again I'd just stop, sit down, and take in the country.

West were the Needle Mountains and north the Grenadiers, some of the highest mountains in the country. One of the Needles was Mt. Eolus, over fourteen thousand feet, and I'd no idea that more than twenty years in the future two men would stake a mining claim atop that mountain and name it for *The Daybreakers*, a novel I would write.

For a few wonderful days I climbed, hiked, watched bears through my binoculars, and sat up high where the eagles were; and sometimes, looking into the vast canyon below, I could look down upon eagles, flying far below where I sat.

Years later I would stand at Overlook Point and look again at these same mountains, but from a different angle. From where we stood we could look down at Emerald Lake and east toward Silver Mesa and Virginia and Missouri Gulches.

The mesas were very green that year except where ice had polished the white rock as smooth as a woman's thigh, a marvelous contrast of color. Always I leave such scenes with reluctance and each time wonder if I shall ever return again to that very place. All too rarely have I returned.

We drove that day past acres of columbine and found a precarious way back to the highway. Later, in Silverton, having coffee in the Bent Elbow I looked toward the mountains and wondered what it must have been like when the boom was on and men like Bat Masterson and Wyatt Earp were stopping by, possibly spending time in the very room where I sat.

Nor did I have to wonder too much, for I had been in boom towns myself, although of a later vintage. Silverton lay cupped in the mountains, as did Ouray, further along over the Million Dollar Highway. The basin in which Silverton lay had originally been called Baker Park, named for Captain Charles Baker, who camped there in 1861 while exploring for minerals.

There are stories everywhere—lost mines, hidden treasures, and best of all, the mountains themselves. Of course, there is the sudden and the unexpected. One night shortly before another of my visits, there was such an occasion. One of the mines was working an ore body too close to the bottom of a lake and suddenly in the middle of the night, the bottom gave way, a space about the length of two football fields, and the entire lake dropped through the mine. Water shot from the tunnel as from a gigantic hose, carrying timbers, tools, and boulders.

An old friend of mine, Sheriff Virgil Mason, was making his rounds and had just driven past the mine when the accident took place. Virgil told the story to Dr. John McHale, the futurist, and me, while standing alongside our car in the ghost town of Animas Forks.

On the slope above us was the house where Tom Walsh, father of Evelyn Walsh McLean, who owned the Hope Diamond, is reported to have lived.

It was coming on to rain and we got into our four-wheel-drive cars and drove back down the trail to Silverton, and hot coffee. Both Virgil and Dr. John are gone now, and I miss them still. They were good men.

pages 142-143: Aspen grove in the San Juan Mountains, Colorado.
page 145: Contorted Bristlecone pine; Sangre de Cristo Range, Colorado.
above: Cumberland Basin, La Plata Mountains, Colorado.

A PLACE FOR EAGLES

When morning came I walked upon the mountain. The sky was very blue and there were no clouds, although if the pattern held true there would be clouds and perhaps a brief shower before the afternoon was gone.

The forest lay just below, only a few yards away, but here above the timberline there were no trees except for a few dwarfed Engelmann spruce that had won a precarious grip upon the tundra. If the climate proved favorable they might, over many years, push a little deeper.

This was the place where rivers began, flowing from under the slide rock in small cold streams only a few inches wide. I drank from one of the streams and squatting beside it watched a yellow-bellied marmot watching me. Although I meant him no harm he was not at all sure of me and disappeared among the rocks, no doubt irritated by my unexpected intrusion into his neighborhood.

149

It was very still, and I liked it that way. I was in the domain of wild creatures, and while expecting to see few of them I was quite sure they would see me. Often in the past I had followed bears with my binoculars, enjoying their activities, and sometimes I had even trailed them at a safe distance. They undoubtedly knew I was there, but they ignored me as long as I kept my distance, which I never failed to do. These were black bears, however. I would never try it with a grizzly. In fact, if I saw a grizzly or one's tracks I would leave promptly, making some tracks of my own.

I would not want to kill a grizzly—there are too few of them left. Nor would I wish to be killed by one, and no grizzly would be as tolerant as a black bear. He would be very likely to lie down beside his trail to see what manner of creature had the temerity to follow him, and he would be very likely to simply erase this human mistake from his path before going on to more important matters.

The trail I walked was an ancient trail holding to the high country above the canyons. It was easier to walk here at almost eleven thousand feet than down below where one was continually climbing in and out of canyons or weaving a way around or over deadfalls and brush. Here it was wide open country under a wide open sky, with a few bronze- or copper-toned peaks reaching up toward it.

Far off, perhaps fifty miles away, there was a serrated line of peaks, some of them still snow covered. They were mountains I knew well, several of them fourteeners, of which Colorado has more than its share. The air was clear and cool. Here and there in shaded places there were patches of last winter's snow, and glancing up I detected movement on one of the high, rocky ridges. When I put my glasses on the spot I sighted several elk crossing the ridge by what was obviously an often used trail. Steep as it was, and hundreds of feet higher than where I stood, they seemed to have no problem. For several minutes I watched, then walked on to a place I knew.

It was a small bench, almost perfectly level with a few trees at one end and backed by a steep bank about four feet high. Nearby, one of

page 148: Cathedral spires; Black Hills, South Dakota.
page 149: Front Range, north from Mount Evans, Colorado.
page 151: Entrada sandstone fins and La Sal Mountains, southern Utah.

the streams that came from under the slide rock had found its way, falling in a small waterfall to a bench below. Scattered over the bench were the ashes of several campfires, all built within the past few years. Yet where you would build a fire would be the same spot chosen by someone else. Anyone making a camp would, if possible, choose a place with shelter from the wind, with water and fuel close by. This spot had it all and probably was no different a hundred or even a thousand years ago.

An Indian or still more primitive man seeking a place to camp needed just what you or I might need today. Below the surface there might be charcoal from other fires, and the trail I followed to get here could have been followed in just the same way a thousand or ten thousand years ago. It has been estimated that down in the flatlands it requires approximately one hundred years to build an inch of soil, adding or subtracting a few years, depending on the nature of the country, the vegetation, and so on. Up here in the high country it would probably take more than twice or three times that, as growth and decay are incredibly slow in the Arctic temperatures that prevail much of the year.

Ancient men walked these trails, and ancient men had to camp, and if one could find one of their camps, eventually one could find them all. Once a single camp had been recognized one would simply have to walk a logical distance along the trail and look for the conditions proper for another camp. With some care and the necessary time one could not only locate the camps but one might find arrowheads, spearpoints, scrapers, and other tools that would indicate something of the nature of these people.

Colorado has these high trails and so does Wyoming, and I have seen them in Idaho and British Columbia. Ancient migration routes? Trade routes? Or simply local trails?

They could be used only in summer, but Indians or other primitive people rarely traveled in the winter. It was much more sensible to sit in one's lodge by the side of a comfortable fire and let the storms rage. There was nothing they wanted enough to make them travel in bad weather.

It increases the enjoyment if one goes to the mountains with some knowledge of them. The changes there are infinitely slow, yet there are changes. In the silences one might hear a trickle of small rocks down a mountainside, a rock loosened by melting frost, perhaps. Trees fall,

Cirque Peak top, Sneffels Range, Colorado.

rocks tumble, there are landslides. Year after year if one returns to the same places one will note few changes, yet changes there have been, and they continue. Cold, heat, wind, and rain are constantly active, and then there are the roots of plants, finding their way into the soil, loosening rocks.

The more one knows about geology and the life-styles of plants and animals the greater is the enjoyment, and to appreciate the actual size of some of the country one needs to get into the mountains. Seen from some distance away their enormity cannot be appreciated. Many times, studying mountains through binoculars even with years of experience I have failed to appreciate either size or distance.

At timberline or above one enters a special world. The air is incredibly clear and fresh. Wildflowers are everywhere, changing with the months, and one can see for great distances. Bare peaks where nothing grows tower above, and there is one I know that is reported to have a vein of gold running through it within a few hundred feet of the top, but with sheer sides all around. The one man who reached it found crumbling rock, and although the samples were rich he would not return. That he reached it at all and returned was sheer luck, and he was smart enough to know it.

There are naturalists who know much more about this than I, but at this altitude wildlife is limited. Yet the marmot who watched me drinking from the stream was not alone. There are many of his kind living among the rocks, and there are others—picas, voles, shrews, mice, and pocket gophers—living a sometimes precarious existence but each contributing in its own way to the world of the high country. In their living and dying they let air and water into the deeper soil, they store seeds and plants that decay, and they eventually add their own bodies to the earth in which they live. I have seen people take potshots at such animals for the sheer pleasure of shooting, but it is a mistake. The world of the high country lives precariously, and each animal, each bird, each plant has a role to fulfill. Once gone, they are not easily replaced. Plants crushed under a car's tire may take many years to recover. The season is cold and the battle for survival unending, and in winter these open green fields that slope up toward the high peaks are covered deep with snow.

Yet I have wandered these mountains and mountains in many other places on several continents, and the memories are always fresh. Over yonder, not very far away, is the trail down which Tell Sackett rode in my story *Treasure Mountain*. He was shot at when coming down that trail. About a half mile away is a cliff over which he almost stepped in the dark, a drop of about twelve hundred feet. Nearby is the bench where his father was killed, a hidden place of rare beauty that I discovered once when eating a picnic lunch nearby.

We were sitting about and talking, but after a bit, eager to see more and know more, I started to walk off into the trees. Suddenly I stopped. The green forest floor fell sharply off for perhaps twelve to fifteen feet and below me was the bench, scattered with a few trees, green, lovely, isolated, yet with space enough to bed down a company of soldiers, and invisible from twenty feet away. On one side the shoulder of the mountain rose steeply, on the other was a vast gulf, half screened by trees, a gulf that was a great interior basin.

The mountains are not only mountains for me because I have peopled the lonely places with characters from my stories. All deserts, mountains, rivers, and lakes are places where stories can happen. But all stories could have happened, and many times I have written stories only to discover that something of the kind did happen where I have written it.

Mountains and deserts breed legends, and for good reason. Things have happened there. In years gone by, crossing either was a problem. Now we drive over in a few hours or minutes, or fly over in less, but then it was an ordeal, finding a pass, often building a road . . . nothing was easy.

One finds a fallen-in cabin, rotting logs, an old prospect hole where someone saw a promising bit of rock and dug into the mountain and then went away. Disappointed?

Perhaps, and perhaps running out of grub or of time before snow fell. Often they found more promising or easier areas elsewhere and never returned. Old mines and tunnels can be deathtraps and are better avoided. Timbers rot and stones loosen with the passage of time, or slides wipe away the path to the tunnel.

Of all the places on earth, I believe I like the high country best, but it is not an easy world. Storms come quickly and violently, lightning stabs at the peaks, and there are few safe places to hide. Under a solitary tree is, of course, the worst place, but damp gullies can be just as bad. When a storm comes it is always better to get down off the mountain, for the lonely peaks tolerate but do not welcome visitors.

To descend into the trees is to enter a different world, a world where all is living and dying. Of course, that is true everywhere, but in the wilderness it is ever-present—trees are falling, their trunks decaying, their bark adding to the earth beneath. Lichen eat at the rocks, turning their granite into soil where things may grow.

The world of the high country is one of rare beauty, so lovely, lonely, and wonderful a place. Be kind to it.

As Robinson Jeffers said, "When the cities lie at the monster's feet, there are left the mountains."

---

pages 154-155: Sunrise; Grand Teton Range, Wyoming.

T H E   O L D   O N E S

Their popular name is the Cliff Dwellers, a designation recognized by all. The Navajo referred to them as the Anasazi, a term that means Old Ones. They were a people who occupied much of what is called the Four Corners, an area where Utah, Colorado, Arizona, and New Mexico come together, and Anasazi remains have been found in all four states.

They were on the scene before the time of Christ, and were first known as the Basket Makers. Their first dwellings appear to have been pit houses, atop the mesas or elsewhere, and it was not until later that they descended into the great open caves in the sides of the cliffs at Mesa Verde, Marsh Pass, and other places.

Various reasons have been given for the move into the caves, but the obvious one was security against enemies. Undoubtedly, the caves offered other advantages and presented a challenge to the skills of the builders, but I cannot conceive of any intelligent people climbing in

page 158: Square Tower House, Mesa Verde National Park, Colorado.
page 159: Farview House, Mesa Verde National Park, Colorado.
above: Kiva and Ruins, Mug House; Mesa Verde National Park, Colorado.

and out of those cliffs without some compelling reason. Moreover they had to carry in and store all the corn they grew and what seeds they could gather. In some of the cliff houses there were springs or seeps, but in others water had to be carried up from below or down from the top, no mean feat when it meant climbing or descending ladders while carrying a considerable burden.

That they had already begun to develop their skill as dry farmers is obvious, and judging by the number of grain-storage bins that have been found, their crops must have been adequate to carry them through the winter and until the next harvest time. All planting peoples are subject to the whims of the weather cycle, and the Cliff Dwellers made every effort both to prepare for spells of drouth or rain and to work magic that would control the weather. Yet people who live in settlements have always been the prey of the nomad; not only did their families have to be protected, but the stored grain as well. Scattered in their fields or hunting and gathering they were in no position to resist a sudden onslaught.

There has been much speculation as to what happened to the Anasazi. Why, after so much effort in building, did they abandon their homes and move away?

I do not believe there is only one reason. Undoubtedly, being subject to attack by nomads, of which the first scouting parties of the Navajo-Apache were probably a part, was a factor. Drouth was another, and we know that about the time of their disappearance the Four Corners area was enduring a drouth that lasted twenty or more years. The dwindling fuel supply was still another, and game was probably becoming scarce.

Despite the relative security of their cliff houses, they could not have been happy to see strangers gathering the crops so diligently tended or to realize how many cold, hungry months would follow. The larger houses may have had sufficient numbers of people to defend themselves, but the smaller, outlying places would surely have been vulnerable.

It was not until recently that the size of the Anasazi community was realized. Mesa Verde, Chaco Canyon, Marsh Pass, and a few other areas had been studied, but it is now apparent that the ruins extend over hundreds of square miles. Although several cultures may be involved, and a greater spread of time than was at first believed, it is obvious that we are only beginning to comprehend the extent of the inhabited area.

The archaeological community has moved with care to examine, excavate, and record, a process that must be slow and painstaking. Unhappily, pot hunters, ignorant of the harm they do, have disturbed and looted many sites despite the penalties the law applies if they are caught. An artifact removed from its place loses much of its value; it can be properly judged only in relation to other aspects of the site—where it was found, how it was found, at what level, and so on.

The story of the southwest has only begun to unfold, and what we have thus far discovered is only a few scratchings on the surface of what remains.

I have walked where the Old Ones walked, and followed paths made by their feet. I have drunk from the springs where they knelt to drink, but I have left no mark of my passing, save what occurs in the pages of what I have written. This was their land; it is now, for the moment, our land. It will someday be the land of those who follow, who in better or worse times must take a living from it or find pleasure in its loneliness, its silence, its beauty. I hope to leave no more mark than the passing of a soft wind, to disturb the sand no more, or bend the grass.

Except, here or there I shall plant a tree.

---

page 163: Gila Cliff Dwellings National Monument, New Mexico.
pages 164-165: Farview House, Mesa Verde National Park, Colorado.

COME BACK COUNTRY

The sun was setting and shadows gathering in the canyons and under the towering cliffs. The air was cool after the day's heat, and I gathered sticks to build a fire. Nearby were the sprawled remains of a dead cedar, resembling a giant tarantula.

Bringing the fuel to the shelter offered by some boulders where the wind, if it came up during the night, would not scatter my fire, I built carefully. First a part of an old packrat's nest, then some dead twigs, and finally the cedar. In minutes I had a fire going and water for coffee.

I was alone. My companion, who prospected when time permitted, had gone off toward the Sweet Alice Hills. He would return tomorrow or the day after. If he did not return I'd know he was in trouble, but he was a careful man, used to rough country.

Camp cooking had never been one of my skills, and when venturing into wild country I carried as little weight as possible. My food was

167

usually dried fruit, nuts, or a packet of hard candy. The candy alleviated thirst and was a source of energy.

The fire I built was for comfort and coffee, which I made in a small pot that held two cups. Often when hiking alone I went a whole day without taking time to eat, waiting until the mood struck me or I found a situation that invited stopping.

We had parted in Babylon Pasture, and he had taken a trail along North Elk Ridge toward Beef Basin, but was turning off before getting into the basin to take a trail that led to Sweet Alice Springs. With luck we would meet there, but I was taking a rougher route down the Peavine to Dark Canyon. Not far from the spring, there was a good place to climb out which I had used once before when I had taken the route down Woodenshoe Canyon.

My temporary camp was on a small bench above the Peavine. Camping in the bottom of a canyon was not one of the things I did. There was too much chance of a flash flood with rain that might have fallen miles away and would give no warning until one heard the roar of the onrushing water. By then, unless one had an easy way out of the canyon, it would be too late.

Water runs off these slopes of solid rock like off a tin roof, and it gathers in the canyons to make a rushing stream, a torrent that can last anywhere from a few minutes to several hours. I've seen a few flash floods from two to six feet high, but I've been down canyons where one could see driftwood and broken brush left thirty feet above the canyon floor.

Fifty years ago there were a few cattle in that country, and probably cowhands rode around occasionally. At no time did I see over five or six head, and they had been near Twin Spring, not far from the head of Woodenshoe.

The night was still. My fire flickered against the boulders, and the stars were very bright. Somewhere a stone rattled, fell, then hit another rock much further down. I was carrying a ground sheet and one blanket. Near the fire was a stretch of sand, and I smoothed it before

---

page 166: Rimrock; Deadhorse Point State Park, Utah.
page 167: Spring storm; Oak Creek Canyon, Arizona.
page 169: Balanced rocks and La Sal Mountains, Arches National Park, Utah.

spreading my bed. A blanket around my shoulders, I added cedar to the fire and finished my second cup of coffee. Far away a meteor streaked across the sky, flared briefly, and vanished.

Twice I awakened to add fuel to the fire, and at dawn, when the first vague light appeared, I made coffee again and ate a handful of nuts while the fire was dying. Carefully, then, I scattered sand over the coals, despite the fact that I was on bare rock with nothing to burn within fifty yards.

There was a vague suggestion of a trail into Peavine Canyon, and I took it, picking my way, for there had been rock falls, and in places the trail was almost wiped away. The morning was brisk, but I knew what the day would bring and wished to get into the depths of the canyon, where there would be shade.

Dark Canyon, which lay ahead, was a narrow cleft in the rock with sheer walls that towered at least two thousand feet above the intermittent creek along its bottom. The deepest, darkest part of the canyon would be below the place where I intended to climb out, but I had seen it before.

Here and there were signs of ancient Indians—bits of broken pottery, a straw sandal, a broken arrowhead. Pools of water were

scattered along the bottom of the canyon, with occasional stretches of water forty or fifty feet long; then the stream, if such it could be called, disappeared into the sand. Twice I found trickles of water from springs flowing from cracks in the rock.

It was a quiet, lovely place. Peavine is one of a network of canyons all emptying into Dark Canyon, which in turn drains its waters into the Colorado. It is an immense chasm, and where it reaches the Colorado the cliffs tower a full two thousand feet above the canyon floor and are probably no more than one hundred feet apart. The name Dark Canyon was given for this reason, for except at midday the canyon is in darkness or shadow most of the time.

Yet just below where the Peavine joins the larger canyon the latter widens somewhat, and when bathed in sunlight the walls reveal themselves in bands of tan, rust, and white, splashed with the vivid green of pines and junipers, which grow wherever they can find a place to sink their roots. The delicate shadings of color along the walls offer themselves in a magnificent gallery of changing light and pastel shading.

It was early morning, and I was in no hurry. Walking along slowly, I twice startled deer that ran off a few yards and then stopped to inspect this rare intruder. After I walked on a bit, they returned to feeding, keeping only a casual eye on my progress.

In a cool, shadowed alcove I paused to drink from a spring, watching the sunlight on the cottonwood leaves. The variety of plant growth in Dark Canyon is amazing: there were willows, box elder (I could not recall seeing any since leaving my home in North Dakota), and ash.

At one place where there was a wide pool, almost covering the canyon floor, I found the tracks of many small animals and birds that had come here to drink. There were bees gathering honey from an astonishing variety of flowers, and I saw several hummingbirds.

At noon I stopped to rest at a narrow recess in the wall where ferns dripped down over the rocks. Here, too, was a spring. Looking about I thought how little this had changed since visited in 1871 by Stephen Vandiver Jones. The reason was obvious, for the place is not easy of access, and I hope it remains so.

Rising after a bit, I strolled on down the canyon, climbing over rocks and fallen trees, worming my way through thick stands of brush or willows, the cottonwoods rustling in the slightest breeze. A marmot whistled from a pile of fallen rock, and I whistled back at him. Startled, he paused to look at me; surprised, I suspect, at something that whistled back or perhaps annoyed by my poor imitation.

Peavine emerged into Dark Canyon with only a small change in the surroundings. This is, I believe, one of the most beautiful canyons I have seen, and at no time did I see any sign that men had been here before me. Stephen Vandiver Jones and his companions were only in the lower end of the canyon, but they, too, had exclaimed at its beauty.

It was growing dusk when I finally reached the place where I would climb out, and I looked up at the canyon wall with no enthusiasm. Had I really climbed that? Could I do it again? And why did I get myself into situations like this?

The way out was up a small branch canyon, and the side wall of the canyon could have been no less than twelve hundred feet. There had been a way, precarious but present. Yet with continuing erosion and rock falls the footholds I had once used might be gone. There had been a way up used by Indians, but it had been difficult and unused for perhaps five hundred years.

The start was marked by a certain boulder and a tree, but it required most of an hour, climbing with hands and feet, then walking slanting ledges, to work my way slowly up. Several times I seemed defeated, but at last I topped out only a few yards from the trail my friend would have followed had he reached Sweet Alice Spring.

At the top the sun was still shining over the top of the low mountains to the west, beyond the Colorado.

I smelled smoke before reaching the spring, and when I saw the fire my friend was standing beside it, a long fork in his hand. He had coffee on and bacon frying.

One thing was obvious. If you don't like to take the time for camp cooking, it is always well to go to the mountains with somebody who does.

"Find what you wanted?" I asked.

He waved the fork. "This is it. The trouble is no matter how much you see it is never enough. I've got to come back."

"I know," I agreed. "That's why I call it Come Back Country. Everybody wants to."

---

pages 170-171: Delicate Arch and sandstone bowl, Arches National Park, Utah.
page 172: Sage, clay and sandstone; Lukachukai Mountains, Arizona.
page 175: Sandstone forms above Glen Canyon, Arizona.

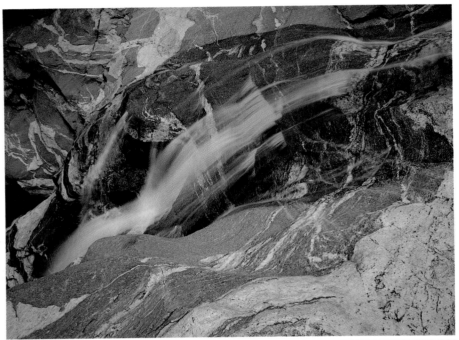

P R O S P E C T I N G

It is all very well to say that gold is where you find it, but from a practical standpoint it is better to begin looking where it is likely to be. A knowledge of geology is a help, but some of the most successful prospectors were men who acquired their knowledge of gold-likely country by knowing a few simple things about how gold comes to be where it is found.

Of course, if one listens to the stories one will immediately realize the first thing is to get a burro. Less gold is being found these days, when prospectors ride in jeeps. Serious prospecting began to decline when the jeep replaced the burro. Having heard all the stories I have no idea how anybody can discover a gold mine without a burro.

Rising after a good night's sleep the prospector will find his burro has wandered off, as given the slightest opportunity, it will. The prospector starts to look for his burro.

Finding a burro is rarely difficult, catching it is another story. This long-eared son of Satan, often called the Arizona canary or the Rocky Mountain mockingbird, will feed complacently until one begins to draw close. Then he will walk off a few steps and begin feeding again, flipping a long ear at an occasional fly. This is standard operating procedure for burros. Indifferent as he may seem he is actually keeping an eye on you, and as you begin to draw near the burro trots off a few steps. A few minutes of this and the most restrained prospector becomes furious. He rushes at the burro, trips, and falls on his face, and as he starts to rise . . . *gold!*

Right there in front of him is a gold-bearing ledge seamed with the bright challenge of wire gold!

Or it may be that, exasperated, one picks up a chunk of rock to throw at the burro, the rock seems unusually heavy. You look again, and there it is.

Gold!

As these methods may seem somewhat impractical, it is best to have some knowledge of erosion and how it works upon the land. Flash floods, wind, rain, and frost are continually at work, as are the roots of trees and other plants. The surface is constantly undergoing change, and any such change may reveal a vein of gold or the particles carried away from it. The specific gravity of sand found in a desert wash is about 2.6; that of placer gold, about 19.3. Obviously, the heavier gold will tend to sink to the bottom and if carried along by the rapid current of a flash flood will tend to fall to the bottom, where the speed of the current decreases, such as the inside of a curve in the stream. At the outer edge of the bend the water is usually moving at good speed, but a sandbar is apt to form on the inside of the bend.

Gold deposited there will, in time, sink as far down as it can go, which means to the bedrock, and even into cracks in the bedrock. Finding gold, a prospector will usually work upstream, trying to find the outcropping that is the source of the gold. In the first chapter of my book *The Empty Land* I tell how at least one such discovery was made.

<hr>

page 176: Head frame; Victor, Colorado.
page 177: Gentle cascade on metamorphic rock; Bear Canyon, Santa Catalina Mountains, Arizona.
page 179: Miners cabin; Independence Pass, Colorado.

Prospecting entails much more than this brief sketch can tell about; books have been written about the practice—but I must insist upon the importance of the burro.

At one time in a western trial an attorney was trying to disqualify a so-called expert witness. He asked the witness how long he had been a prospector, and the witness replied, "Thirty years." The attorney pursued his inquiry and then returned to the question, "How much prospecting did you say you had done?" The witness replied, "Five years."

"But a few minutes ago you said you had been a prospector for thirty years!"

"Yessir, I been a prospector for thirty years. I prospected five years. I spent the other twenty-five lookin' for my burro!"

Undoubtedly he qualified as an expert witness.

The most contented prospector I ever knew was a man I met beside the road in the mountains not far from Hannegan's Meadows, in Arizona.

He was a tall, lean old man who had stopped his jeep beside the road, as I had, and was looking over the country. He was an ex-cowboy and had once worked for French over at Alma, New Mexico. I asked him if he had known Jim Lowe, and he replied that he had. We talked of Jim for several minutes before I realized that he did not know *who* Jim Lowe was; he thought of him merely as a very expert cowboy. When I told him that Jim Lowe was a name used by Butch Cassidy he was astonished, but comparing notes and descriptions we soon identified a couple of the other cowboys as Elza Lay and Harvey Logan, others of the gang that rode with Butch.

As I have said, this tall old man was the most contented prospector I have ever known, and he had worked the science of prospecting into a major art form.

He would drive his jeep into the woods on a beautiful mountain slope where there was a good view. He would park the jeep and check to be sure his gold pan, pick, and shovel were handy; then he would take a fifth of Bourbon and sit under a tree looking out over that vast and beautiful pine forest country of east central Arizona—just sit there, sipping Bourbon from time to time, peacefully contemplating the countryside. Occasionally, he would doze, and then awaken to see how the shadows had moved. He would study the country anew, sip a bit more Bourbon, and check the visible ridges and outcroppings. When it began to grow late he would climb back into his jeep, check to be sure he hadn't left any tools or bottles lying about, and then drive home.

His prospecting had found him happiness, contentment in a land that he loved, and no worries.

A few days before I met him he had celebrated his ninety-fourth birthday.

Then there were Peterson and The Yukon Kid. British Columbia was one of the places where gold was found and a few lucky ones found a lot of it. I first learned that in a mining-camp bunkhouse from these two old-timers, both pushing seventy and working to get a road stake to travel back into British Columbia again.

Our mine superintendent knew them well, and each of them had made it big on at least three occasions. Once in the Yukon in the rush of '98 and the second time in British Columbia. The third time they hit it was in Brazil—"it was gold from the grass roots down" but it was blackwater fever country. You got in and got out in a hurry or you died.

Peterson and The Yukon Kid rode out with $160,000 in gold and they camped on the outskirts of a small town. A soldier came with word they were to report to the *alcalde* or whatever the local official was called. They were sure their gold would be confiscated and they would be thrown in jail, so the Yukon Kid sent word back that they would be riding through town with their Winchesters across their saddle bows and if anybody wanted to arrest them to come and try.

It was a bluff, but Peterson and The Kid were tough men, and they were believed. They got out with their gold.

They didn't gamble money away, and neither was a drinker. They liked getting the gold and they liked spending it, but they spent at leisure, living it up in fine hotels with the best of whatever money could buy. Often the gold would last them a year, sometimes two or three years, and then back to the mines again.

---

page 180: Henson Creek Canyon, San Juan Mountains, Colorado.
page 183: Rock facade, Mother Lode country; Merced River Canyon, California.

When they left the mine where I met them they were headed for Kamloops in British Columbia.

They talked of the towns and the rivers, of Barkerville, Quesnelle Forks, Kamloops, the Fraser River and the Cariboo Road. They were men who loved the wild country and the wild towns; they loved the sheer beauty of it and the strength. They loved the clean fresh air of the mountains, the rushing streams, the hard life, and they were lucky.

Lucky and smart. They did not walk blindly into the country hoping for the best. They knew the kind of ground where gold was apt to be, and each had a fabulous memory for creeks and placers. While they worked one placer they had in mind several others they considered as good.

British Columbia had its share of boom camps, and now of ghost towns. They talked of rivers such as the Stikine, the Liard and the Pease, of creeks like the Tahltan and the McDame. We worked the same shift in the mine. The Kid was running a machine; Peterson and I were mucking and tramming. They liked what they had done and loved talking about the country and where they found the gold and how. Along with their stories there were others, of other miners, other creeks, other towns.

The greatest stories ever told are those around campfires, in bunkhouses, or in ship's fo'c'stles with a bunch of wandering men. They'll have dropped their anchors in forgotten coves and paddled canoes up nameless creeks, and the best of their stories are always for each other, for the ones who have not known the life will not believe what they are hearing.

Whatever happened to Peterson and The Kid? I do not know. There was a postcard a couple of years later from the Dorchester, in London. "We've been living it up for six months, too long at our age. We're going back. There's a creek that empties into the Nahanni . . ."

---

page 185: Eyes of a ghost—adobe ruins; Pearce, Arizona.

TO WALK A DESERT MILE

The outcropping of red rock was not over a half mile away and the morning was cool, the sun not yet above the horizon. Long ago I had learned that any conspicuous landmark had been used as such by others before me, and often they left some indication of their passing. I would go a half mile out and a half mile back and then drive to the ranch for breakfast.

Around me on the desert floor lay a scattering of stones and pebbles, dark with desert varnish. Turning one over with my toe I exposed its gray underside, which was the natural color of the rock. The upper surface was dark and polished. Desert varnish is a surface stain of iron or manganese oxide, black to brown in color and caused by the sun's action on the rock. How long it takes to form is a much debated question.

The place where I stood was on the shoreline of an ancient lake or sea that had once covered more than two thousand square miles of the desert floor. Several times the basin had filled and several times dried up, leaving only the line of the old beach along the cliffs and scattered shells to mark its passing.

Stooping, I picked up one of the shells, worn tissue thin by the action of wind and wave. It crumbled in my fingers, leaving only a few pearllike fragments and dust. How old had it been? Five hundred years? A thousand? More?

Turning my back to the basin, I faced the raw-backed, serrated ridges, almost devoid of growth. Picking my way among the scattered rocks I started toward the red outcropping, standing like a sentinel just beyond a small butte. A lizard darted from beneath a creosote bush, paused an instant to study me, then vanished around a rock. A flock of Gambel's quail bustled away, topknots bobbing. Only a few took to the air, sailing away a dozen yards or so to join the others.

It was very still, and my soft-soled boots made almost no sound upon the sand or rocks. I liked the fragrance of the creosote bushes and wondered again at their regular spacing. Viewed from the air they resemble an orchard, so neat is their arrangement, which is the plant's method of assuring itself sufficient water. I have heard that their roots poison any plant that tries to grow too close, but this obviously does not include burro bush, which often grows among the creosote.

Desert plants, like desert animals, have learned how to survive, some developing a hard, shiny surface on the upper side of their leaves so as to yield little moisture to the sun. Others have fluted columns, such as the saguaro, or are covered with needles, such as the varieties of cholla. The needles provide some protection from the sun but also assure the plants' distribution by sticking to anything that passes.

There are animals, such as the kangaroo rat, that survive without water. When offered water they do not drink. Their metabolism is geared to conserving moisture rather than excreting it.

page 186: Mountain Palm Oasis, Anza Borrego Desert State Park, California.
page 187: Agave and cholla; Anza Borrego Desert State Park, California.
page 189: Octillo in bloom; Anza Borrego Desert State Park, California.

Without the desert man would be hard put to reconstruct his past. The processes of destruction are infinitely slower in the desert, and desert or semidesert has preserved some of our earliest remains, allowing us to explore the ruins of ancient cities. The ability of the desert to preserve is little short of miraculous. In the Taklamakan Desert, of Sinkiang, China, there was discovered some years ago the oldest piece of paper known. It was dated 130 A.D., if I recall correctly, and the art of making paper had come into existence only in 106 A.D. The paper was intact, and the words could be deciphered.

The Taklamakan is incredibly dry, so dry that in much of the desert wood does not rot, and sections of carved wood have been found lying face down in the sand relatively undamaged after hundreds of years.

The more we learn of the world the more we should be cautious about our statements on the past. So much of what we believe is theory or founded upon theory, and much of such theory is based on insufficient evidence. The great danger lies in accepting a theory for fact and building mountains of learning on insecure foundations.

One has to begin somewhere and a theory is such a place, but a theory can be a trap and is not to be trusted too much.

Picking my way through the rocks I walked toward the red outcropping, taking my time. Over to my left several paloverde trees made a lacy green pattern of their branches against the rock.

The red outcropping proved larger than it had appeared, and I climbed part way up its side to look around. A deep wash, cut by runoff water from the mountains, lay along one side, but what took my eye was a path, a trail if you like, taking off from near the base of the outcropping. From where I stood I could see it winding among the rocks and cactus and obviously leading the way into the mountains.

Had the Indians who made that trail used the outcropping to locate it? I had no doubt.

Glancing back the way I had come, I hesitated. Back there lay breakfast, a hot cup of coffee, and my work, yet I have rarely been able to refuse a trail. Crossing the wash I stood upon the trail. "Trail,"

below: Yaqui Pass, Anza Borrego Desert State Park, California.
page 193: Borrego Badlands, Anza Borrego Desert State Park, California.
page 195: Mountain Palms Oasis, Anza Borrego Desert State Park, California.

incidentally, is a word that was used mostly in the western part of the country. In the east and in the Appalachians they were called paths, and long before the coming of the white man warpaths and trading paths crisscrossed the country.

Well, I would just walk a little way, I thought. There was a hill just ahead. I would walk just that far. An hour later and several miles higher upon the mountain, I looked back. My plan to walk a desert mile had gone glimmering, as I had been drawn on by the ancient trail. Around me were several clumps of ocotillo, a canelike plant covered with very impressive thorns. Sometimes called candlewood, it burns with a hot flame and gives off an intensely black smoke. Rarely does one come upon a dead ocotillo, for it seems to have learned how to survive. A brief shower causes the plant to leaf out and often to bloom with brilliant red blossoms. The Cahuilla used to make a drink of these blossoms, and they also ate the seeds.

A coyote had crossed my path, probably not over an hour ago, and certainly since I began my walk. No doubt he was somewhere along the mountainside, watching me. A bighorn, probably down to drink from an irrigation ditch, had used this trail also. As I glanced back again, the valley lay clear and bright in the sunlight. Far off, a car turned a corner and sunlight flashed from its windshield, a car that was, perhaps, four miles away, but it could be a thousand years away in time.

This was the desert. Down there was what we call civilization. Suppose a rock rolled under my foot and I fell? One need not fall far to break bones or even a back. One could lie here within sight of those distant houses down there, and one could die of the injury or of thirst. I had seen no other human tracks on the trail I followed. No one had come this way, perhaps, in months, even years.

Why should they? The rocks were barren. The climb was steady, the footing was not good, and apparently there was nothing to see.

The sun was up now, and it was warm. Soon it would be hot, over one hundred degrees. By midday it would be up to one hundred and ten, but on the ground it would be much hotter, perhaps one hundred and thirty to forty degrees. Fortunately I never go into the desert without a canteen; without water a man might last two days, perhaps three. One goes gently into the desert, aware always that death lies waiting. Not expecting, just waiting. The desert makes no allowance for carelessness.

Already I had walked further than intended, but where did the trail lead? Obviously others had followed it. I had no doubt it had been an Indian trail originally, but a white man had done work here and there, probably to turn the old Indian trail into a bridle path. I walked on.

The growth was changing, a subtle change but visible to a discerning eye. There was no paloverde now, no ocotillo, although still occasional barrel cactus and cholla. I glimpsed an evergreen buckthorn, a plant used by Indians to provide a deep yellow dye. Usually it was found in the juniper areas of the mountains. The day was very hot.

Pausing, I turned to look back. The valley was lost in haze. No individual buildings were visible, although the roads were still to be seen in the places where they were closest to the mountains.

A golden eagle soared on motionless wings, riding the thermals. High as he was and insignificant as I must seem, I knew he was interested in me. I was not listed in his table of possible food items but nevertheless I was important to him because my walking might startle small creatures into movement and so expose them to his attack. Nothing happens in the wilderness without repercussions.

Another mile, and still another. By now my wife would know what had happened, and whatever breakfast had been prepared would have been put aside until later.

The trail followed the easy contours of the mountain, rising steadily but not abruptly. Animals and Indians, unless startled, do not waste strength in climbing straight up. They are wise enough to conserve their strength and accept the easy way.

Twice I saw lizards, once a small gopher, but no snakes. So many people worry about snakes in the desert, but snakes do not like heat; they prefer shady places, and one should avoid stepping too close to the shade under bushes, trees, and rocks. Rarely have I come upon snakes in the desert. They are there, of course, but are nocturnal creatures and avoid man when possible. Nevertheless, one should walk with caution and not stoop to pick up anything from the ground without a careful look around, and, of course, be careful to notice whether that stick you are reaching for is really a stick and not a snake.

At one time I was in the desert for several months and saw nothing resembling a snake until the last day. A very pretty young lady offered to drive me to a mine to pick up my traveling gear, and on the way out and back we ran over three snakes, all headed in the same direction. Some snake convention, no doubt.

Now, suddenly, the trail dipped down into a small fold in the hills and I stopped, amazed.

Before me was an oasis of palms, at least two or three hundred of them tucked away in the hills out of sight. This, then, was where the trail led.

There was no sign of man. The palms were cloaked from top to bottom in skirts of old palm leaves, leaving each tree ten to twelve feet in diameter.

All was very still. No bird moved. Nothing. I walked warily, not knowing what animal might start up or what else I might find. There was no water visible. It is often said that a palm tree has its head in the sun and its feet in the water, and it is true that where one finds palms, water is not far below the surface.

Once in the grove I stopped, listening. In the wilderness, and particularly in the desert, one finds oneself often pausing to listen . . . to what?

There was no sound, only stillness. A faint wind stirred the dry palm fronds, a small creature rustled among the dead leaves at the base of a palm. I moved on, working my way through the grove toward the center.

Suddenly, I stopped short, my hair prickling on the back of my head.

There, her back to me, dirty blonde-gray hair falling over a shawl of dry, dead palm leaves, and seated on a fallen palm log, sat the witch that haunted this place. I scarcely breathed, then slowly I relaxed.

It was not a witch. Not really. It was the stump of a fallen palm, broken off by wind—a sight rarely seen—covered by palm leaves and looking very much as described. I had a camera and took a picture. The witch did not move. Nothing stirred. Edging around through the palms and brush I looked at her from the front.

No face and no features, the streaky blonde-gray hair covered where the face would have been. There was an opening . . . was she peering at me?

Satisfied that I had found the spirit of this lonely place I walked away.

I did not look back.

THE PACIFIC COAST

For how many thousands of years did it lie alone? How long did the great gray waves batter at its granite shore, its sandy beaches, its clay cliffs? How long did it wait for men to come with their dreams, their ships?

We know too little, far too little. History is a gigantic jigsaw puzzle with most of the pieces missing. Juan Rodríguez Cabrillo came in 1542 to explore for Spain, and died, adding his flesh and bones to the earth of the coast of the Pacific.

Then came the great treasure galleons from the Philippines, sailing to Acapulco laden with gold, silk, and spices for Spain. Close upon them came Frances Drake and his *Golden Hind*, a small wolf seeking a fat prey, and then came Vizcaino, exploring the coast to seek a haven for the treasure galleons where they might take on fresh water and refit for such as Drake and his men.

To Vizcaino came an Indian woman with some pieces of figured Chinese silk which had come from a ship wrecked upon those shores long before. A ship from where? Manned by whom?

In one period of about fifty years, forty-one Chinese, Japanese, and Korean vessels drifted to our shores from Acapulco to Alaska, so how many might there have been before any records were kept?

Almost every mile of that long coast from Alaska to the end of Baja has its stories of shipwreck and disaster. The Indians had stories of shipwrecked sailors whom they killed and of at least one who was found to be a worker with metals and who was kept alive because of his skills. Points Arguello and Conception, Cape Mendocino, all were graveyards of good ships broken up on the rocks or trapped in treacherous sands from which there was no escape.

Who first found his way to that not so pacific coast we do not know. We do know that Bering had a chart before he "discovered" the strait named for him, and we know a chart existed covering the west coast from Alaska at least as far as the northern tip of Vancouver Island. Certainly, judging by the evidence of charts and wrecks alone, all the seas of the world must have been sailed in unrecorded voyages.

From my San Pedro days I remember best the tough old steam schooners that carried freshly cut lumber down the coast from Grays Harbor, Coos Bay, Aberdeen, and those other timber towns along the Northwest Coast.

These were not the slim white passenger ships with rows of portholes along each side, with promenade decks and brass fittings, nor were they the slender, graceful yachts or the freighters that came and went from Pacific ports carrying merchandise to the world. The steam schooners were tough old work ships, wide in the beam, deep in the hold, battered and weather-beaten. Their holds were piled deep

page 196: Tillamook head; Ecola State Park, Oregon.
page 197: Battering waves; Ecola State Park, Oregon.
page 199: Rain Forest interior; Ecola State Park, Oregon.

with lumber, but usually they carried a deck load as well. Occasionally in rough weather the deck load would shift and one would see a steam schooner coming into port with a heavy list to one side or another. On at least two occasions I saw one come in lying over on its beam end. But they did their job. They carried the lumber that helped build Los Angeles, San Diego, and a dozen other California cities.

Often they discharged their cargo at the old E. K. Wood lumber dock where Ports o' Call now is. Lying in narrow slips with soft rain falling over their battered, weather-beaten hulls, there was little about them of the romance of the sea.

They are gone now, their crews scattered. Some were dismantled and destroyed, while others were lost at sea or along the coast. The *Yellowstone*, on which I ate a dozen good meals when the going was rough, went down off Humboldt Bar in 1933. The *Trinidad* and the *Halco* were lost also, faded dowagers of the waterfronts that weathered many a rough sea.

Northern California, Oregon, and Washington present some of the most magnificent coasts to be seen anywhere, and each cove or

stretch of beach has its story. At Mohler, a few years ago, a farmer discovered a dozen Spanish coins, all dated around 1648, stirring up again the story of a Spanish galleon wrecked nearby, whether by storms or pirates is still a question.

Cape Blanco, Tillamook Rock, the Columbia Bar, and Cape Flattery . . . there are dozens of stories of each, stories of storm and shipwreck and of heroism and survival. And back of the coasts are the forests, the giant redwoods, the sequoias, and of course, the pines.

The Olympic Mountains, tucked in between Juan de Fuca Strait and Puget Sound are a fantastic area of rain forest, glaciers, plunging waterfalls, and some of the densest forest in North America. First sighted by Juan Perez in 1774, they were given their present name a few years later by a British captain, John Meares.

To follow the lonely paths along the mountains and through the woods is a rare experience. At every turn there is beauty, huge old trees and fallen logs giving themselves to the forest again; and when high enough one can look to the westward to see the Pacific in all its gray majesty under a far-off rainstorm, and south toward Grays Harbor, where those old steam schooners came.

A great granite shoulder of mountain topped with ragged, wind-blown firs, dripping with rain. Clouds low over the mountains, shutting out their peaks, and sunlight over what must be Grays Harbor and several streams running toward it: all this I remember from a momentary pause where a ledge of rock jutted out from the mountain.

A wide-winged bird swings by so swiftly I cannot see what he is—an eagle, I think—and he turns westward toward the sea where the great gray waves are gathering themselves to pound again upon the shore.

I shall leave the mountain now and go back to the towns of men. Envy is no part of my being and has never been, but I envy now. I envy those who saw it first, before a tree had been felled or a town built, when there was only the sea, the long, long shore, and the mountains behind it, only a sun rising or setting or a moon above the water.

---

page 200: Cape Flattery, Washington.
pages 202-203: Rock silhouettes at Cape Flattery, Washington.

THE ETERNAL FRONTIER

The question I am most often asked is, "Where is the frontier now?"

The answer should be obvious. Our frontier lies in outer space.

The moon, the asteroids, the planets, these are mere stepping stones, where we will test ourselves, learn needful lessons, and grow in knowledge before we attempt those frontiers beyond our solar system. Outer space is a frontier without end, the eternal frontier, an everlasting challenge to explorers not alone of other planets and other solar systems but also of the mind of man.

All that has gone before was preliminary. We have been preparing ourselves mentally for what lies ahead. Many problems remain, but if we can avoid a devastating war we shall move with a rapidity scarcely to be believed. In the past seventy years we have developed the automobile, radio, television, transcontinental and transoceanic flight, and the electrification of the country, among a multitude of other such developments. In 1900 there were 144 miles of surfaced road in the

United States. Now there are over 3,000,000. Paved roads and the development of the automobile have gone hand in hand, the automobile being civilized man's antidote to overpopulation.

What is needed now is leaders with perspective; we need leadership on a thousand fronts, but they must be men and women who can take the long view and help to shape the outlines of our future. There will always be the nay-sayers, those who cling to our lovely green planet as a baby clings to its mother, but there will be others like those who have taken us this far along the path to a limitless future.

We are a people born to the frontier. It has been a part of our thinking, waking, and sleeping since men first landed on this continent. The frontier is the line that separates the known from the unknown wherever it may be, and we have a driving need to see what lies beyond. It was this that brought people to America, no matter what excuses they may have given themselves or others.

Freedom of religion, some said, and the need for land, a better future for their children, the lust for gold, or the desire to escape class restrictions—all these reasons were given. The fact remains that many, suffering from the same needs and restrictions, did not come.

Why then did some cross the ocean to America and not others? Of course, all who felt that urge did not come to America; some went to India, Africa, Australia, New Zealand, or elsewhere. Those who did come to America began almost at once to push inland, challenging the unknown, daring to go beyond the thin line that divides the known and the unknown. Many had, after landing from the old country, developed good farms or successful businesses; they had become people of standing in their communities. Why then did they move on, leaving all behind?

I believe it to be something buried in their genes, some inherited trait, perhaps something essential to the survival of the species.

page 204: Yucca plant in Malpais lava beds; Tularosa Valley, New Mexico.
page 205: Stone monument; Black Rock Desert, Nevada.
page 206: Desert ridges; Mount San Jacinto, California.

above: Del Norte Redwoods; Redwood National Park, California.
page 209: North Clear Creek Falls, San Juan Mountains, Colorado.

They went to the edge of the mountains; then they crossed the mountains and found their way through impassable forests to the Mississippi. After that the Great Plains, the Rocky Mountains, and on to Oregon and California. They trapped fur, traded with Indians, hunted buffalo, ranched with cattle or sheep, built towns, and farmed. Yet the genes lay buried within them, and after a few months, a few years, they moved on.

Each science has its own frontiers, and the future of our nation and the world lies in research and development, in probing what lies beyond.

A few years ago we moved into outer space. We landed men on the moon; we sent a vehicle beyond the limits of the solar system, a vehicle still moving farther and farther into that limitless distance. If our world were to die tomorrow, that tiny vehicle would go on and on forever, carrying its mighty message to the stars. Out there, someone, sometime, would know that once we existed, that we had the vision and we made the effort. Mankind is not bound by its atmospheric envelope or by its gravitational field, nor is the mind of man bound by any limits at all.

One might ask—why outer space, when so much remains to be done here? If that had been the spirit of man we would still be hunters and food gatherers, growling over the bones of carrion in a cave somewhere. It is our destiny to move out, to accept the challenge, to dare the unknown. It is our destiny to achieve.

Yet we must not forget that along the way to outer space whole industries are springing into being that did not exist before. The computer age has arisen in part from the space effort, which gave great impetus to the development of computing devices. Transistors, chips, integrated circuits, teflon, new medicines, new ways of treating diseases, new ways of performing operations, all these and a multitude of other developments that enable man to live and to live better are linked to the space effort. Most of these developments have been so incorporated into our day-to-day life that they are taken for granted, their origin not considered.

If we are content to live in the past, we have no future. And today is the past.

page 211: Roadway to nowhere; South Pass, Wyoming.
pages 212-213: Headwaters, Arkansas River; Leadville, Colorado.

ABOUT LOUIS L'AMOUR

*"I think of myself in the oral tradition—as a troubadour, a village
taleteller, the man in the shadows of the campfire. That's the way
I'd like to be remembered—as a storyteller. A good storyteller."*

It is doubtful that any author could be as at home in the world recreated in his novels as Louis Dearborn L'Amour. Not only could he physically fill the boots of the rugged characters he wrote about, but he literally "walked the land my characters walk." His personal experiences as well as his lifelong devotion to historical research combined to give Mr. L'Amour the unique knowledge and understanding of people, events, and the challenge of the American frontier that became the hallmarks of his popularity.

Of French-Irish descent, Mr. L'Amour could trace his own family in North America back to the early 1600s and follow their steady progression westward, "always on the frontier." As a boy growing up in Jamestown, North Dakota, he absorbed all he could about his family's frontier heritage, including the story of his great-grandfather who was scalped by Sioux warriors.

Spurred by an eager curiosity and desire to broaden his horizons, Mr. L'Amour left home at the age of fifteen and enjoyed a wide variety of jobs including seaman, lumberjack, elephant handler, skinner of dead cattle, assessment miner, and an officer in the tank destroyers during World War II. During his "yondering" days he also circled the world on a freighter, sailed a dhow on the Red Sea, was shipwrecked in the West Indies and stranded in the Mojave Desert. He won fifty-one of fifty-nine fights as a professional boxer and worked as a journalist and lecturer. He was a voracious reader and collector of rare books. His personal library contained 17,000 volumes.

Mr. L'Amour "wanted to write almost from the time I could talk." After developing a widespread following for his many frontier and adventure stories written for fiction magazines, Mr. L'Amour published his first full-length novel, *Hondo,* in the United States in 1953. Every one of his more than 100 books is in print; there are nearly 230 million copies of his books in print worldwide, making him one of the bestselling authors in modern literary history. His books have been translated into twenty languages, and more than forty-five of his novels and stories have been made into feature films and television movies.

His hardcover bestsellers include *The Lonesome Gods, The Walking Drum* (his twelfth-century historical novel), *Jubal Sackett, Last of the Breed,* and *The Haunted Mesa.* His memoir, *Education of a Wandering Man,* was a leading bestseller in 1989. Audio dramatizations and adaptations of many L'Amour stories are available on cassette tapes from Bantam Audio Publishing.

The recipient of many great honors and awards, in 1983 Mr. L'Amour became the first novelist ever to be awarded the Congressional Gold Medal by the United States Congress in honor of his life's work. In 1984 he was also awarded the Medal of Freedom by President Reagan.

Louis L'Amour died on June 10, 1988. His wife, Kathy, and their two children, Beau and Angelique, carry the L'Amour tradition forward with new books written by the author during his lifetime to be published by Bantam well into the nineties—among them, three additional Hopalong Cassidy novels: *The Trail to Seven Pines, The Riders of High Ridge,* and *Trouble Shooter.*

ABOUT DAVID MUENCH

David Muench is one of the most respected photographers of the North American wilderness. His sensitivity to, and determination to champion, the strength and beauty of the continent has led to extensive contributions of his work in magazines, books, advertising, wilderness and conservation publications.

Somewhat of a maverick in landscape photography, Mr. Muench has studied under the tutorship of nature, following his own intuitions and perceptions without imitating the work of other photographers. In his own words:

> "The underlying ethos of my directions is to record the spirit of the land, A Spirit of Place, to make what I see so stark and real visually that my photographs express a communication with the universe—and with myself. Traveling and making photographic impressions is my total involvement. Timing, patience in waiting for the right pattern of sun and shadow, for the precise angle of light, or the one moment of proper mood challenges my mind's eye and camera. To photograph in nature allows me to retain a childlike pattern of discovery. and exploration—an inspirational force in my life—sometimes to share and communicate to people the same impressions and feelings I experience. Hopefully my work leads to a celebration of man and the earth—and the mystical forces of nature which help to shape our destinies."

Among the magazines which have featured Mr. Muench's photography are National Geographic, Life, Arizona Highways, and American West. More than thirty books of his photographs have been published, including *Desert Images, Anasazi: Ancient People of the Rock, Lewis and Clark Country, This Great Land, Sierra Nevada, Rocky Mountains, Colorado, New Mexico* and *California.*

In 1975, Mr. Muench was commissioned to provide photographs for 33 large murals on the Lewis and Clark Expedition for the Jefferson Expansion Memorial in St. Louis, Missouri, to include 350 smaller eco-photographs to relate to and accompany the murals. The hanging of this large collection was completed in June 1976.

Mr. Muench resides in Santa Barbara, California with his wife and two children.

LOUIS L'AMOUR
FRONTIER

PHOTOGRAPHS BY
DAVID MUENCH

BANTAM BOOKS
NEW YORK · TORONTO · LONDON · SYDNEY · AUCKLAND

We would like to extend a special acknowledgment
and our thanks
to Irwyn Applebaum, our editor,
and Barbara N. Cohen, our designer,
for their work on *Frontier.*

LOUIS L'AMOUR
DAVID MUENCH

FRONTIER
A Bantam Book
Bantam hardcover edition / November 1984
Bantam trade paperback edition / December 1991

All rights reserved.
Text copyright © 1984 by Louis & Katherine L'Amour Trust.
Photographs copyright © 1984 by David Muench Photography, Inc.
Book design by Barbara N. Cohen.

No part of this book may be reproduced or transmitted in any form
or by any means, electronic or mechanical, including photocopying,
recording, or by any information storage and retrieval system,
without permission in writing from the publisher.
For information address: Bantam Books.

Library of Congress Catalog Card Number: 84-45178

ISBN 0-553-35390-X

Published simultaneously in the United States and Canada

Bantam Books are published by Bantam Books, a division of Bantam Doubleday
Dell Publishing Group, Inc. Its trademark, consisting of the words "Bantam
Books" and the portrayal of a rooster, is Registered in the United States Patent
and Trademark Office and in other countries. Marca Registrada. Bantam Books,
666 Fifth Avenue, New York, New York 10103.

PRINTED IN THE UNITED STATES OF AMERICA

RAN   0 9 8 7 6 5 4 3 2 1

To Daniel and Ruth Boorstin

L.L'A.

To those who love this land
and work for its preservation—
that we may realize the future
by learning from the past.

D.M.

C O N T E N T S

Opening page: Ponderosa and cabin; White Mountains, Arizona.
Title page: Pounding Mill Overlook, Blue Ridge Parkway, North Carolina.
Contents page: Cascade flow; Rock Creek, Beartooth Range, Montana.
page 1: Snake River and Hell's Canyon, Oregon-Idaho border.

F R O N T I E R

EXTENDING HORIZONS

*F*rontier is a very special book for me.

For more than thirty years in more than two hundred novels and short stories, I have written about many aspects of the American frontier experience—from the courageous explorers and early settlers of the sixteenth century on through the succeeding generations of the builders and shapers who followed them across the continent. However, for a long time I have wanted to temporarily leave behind the boundaries of fiction to share more directly with my readers some of what I have learned and observed about our great North American land during a lifetime of study and appreciation.

This land, which we hold in trust for future generations and which is ours to improve while we live, is a remarkable land. The landscape has enormous variety, which sometimes escapes visitors. In the twenty-five essays that follow I have tried to offer a few brief aspects of the history, geology, excitement, wonder, and overwhelming power of this land.

For some people the term "frontier" may bring to mind only the way west. That is acceptable as long as one remembers that everything from where the Atlantic Ocean breaks upon the shore was west at one time. It was all frontier, and it is the entire breadth of the continent from east to west that I have attempted to deal with in this volume.

In some of these essays I have dealt with aspects of the broad historical movements across the land, such as the pioneers and the wagon trains. At other times I have tried to deal with some of the truly special places of North America, such as the mysterious Outer Banks of the Carolinas and the canyon country of the southwest, with its haunting appeal. I have also drawn from my personal experiences of living with this land, trying to get the reader ever closer to what it feels like to walk a desert mile or to travel above timberline. In each essay I have tried to reveal the enormous impact that this extraordinary land of ours has had—and continues to have—upon the men and women who encounter it.

No writer can possibly convey in words alone the full experience of the land, so I have asked for the assistance of David Muench, a poet with a camera, to help me better illustrate some of what we have both been fortunate to see in the back country. Through the photographs that David and I have selected to accompany each essay we have tried to deepen the reader's appreciation for the territory about which I write. I feel he gets as close as anyone I have ever seen to capturing the spirit of the land through the camera lens.

In many of David's photos one gets glimpses of how this land was first seen in its wild, lonesome state. There is much rough country presented in this book, but there is much beauty as well. However, we must remember that beauty is ever-changing, minute by minute, hour by hour. The passing of a cloud, the changing directions of the sunlight, all of these things present the viewer with scenes that are never twice the same.

page 2: Woods Canyon Lake, Mogollon Rim, Arizona.
page 3: Tallulah River Canyon, Chattahoochee National Forest, Georgia.
page 5: Tumbleweed collection and yucca stalks; Black Range, New Mexico.

Our country was opened up and built by people unwilling to accept the horizons they were offered: they had to push ever forward, trying to go beyond the limits presented to them. They gave themselves many excuses for going—to settle upon new land, to trap for fur, to dig for gold—but their real reason was their wish to extend themselves and to extend their horizons.

It is this that leads men onward in whatever field they attempt; it is the challenge more than the profit. We have been called a materialistic civilization. What other is there? It is man's attempt to better his existence that has brought us to where we are; it is man's attempt to live, and then to live better, that has led to all our progress in law, in medicine, and in material comforts.

Civilization, with all its faults, is man's greatest creation. Above all, it has spawned leisure, not leisure simply to bask in the sun, but leisure to think, to contemplate, to create. That is why the earliest civilizations of which we know developed in the warm climates of Egypt, Sumeria, the Indus Valley, Mexico, Central America, and Peru.

In the cold northern climates man was too busy in his struggle for food, clothing, and fuel to have much time to consider his place in the universe, too busy to give much time to creating art, music, or literature. These things were there, but their development was limited. By the time one has sorted food for the winter, the summer is gone.

Those who came to America were a selected people, selected by themselves. They *chose* to come. They were willing to venture across a sea into a strange world. They had already taken a step beyond; when they walked up the gangplank of the vessel that was to bring them to this continent, they severed ties with the past and stood in the passageway to a future that would demand new ways of living, new ways of thinking, and constant adjustment. They dropped off the old ways as a snake sheds its skin, and the path was open before them. From among these some were willing to take even bigger steps on the land, and they moved out, pushing farther west, into the deep forest, over the mountains.

I am not saying these were better people, only that they were different insofar as they were willing to take the big step. This very move asserted their independence, and as some moved westward that difference was enhanced. On the eastern shore many would always look back to Europe for guidance. American authors such as Poe, Whitman, and Irving were not accepted here until they had been

Fluted erosion; Cathedral Gorge, Nevada.

page 8: Gentle flow of winter; Hondo Canyon, Sangre de Cristo Range, New Mexico.
above: Gypsum forms; White Sands National Monument, New Mexico.
page 11: Evening; Rio Grande River, Texas.

accepted in Europe. There was no such feeling on the frontier, where every onward move meant a cutting of ties.

Our debt to the frontier is great. George Washington as soldier and surveyor and land hunter spent many of his early years on the frontier and in wild country. Thomas Jefferson grew up in a house that was one of the first at which the Long Hunters stopped when they returned to civilization. He must have absorbed many ideas from these visitors, who brought with them not only the romance of the wilderness but their confident independence born from having met the enemy and survived.

There were no easy ways, though. Every advance offered its problems and every problem created its problem solvers. There were no prescribed social levels and no limits for individuals. For instance, the nearest market town was not three miles away, as it might have been in the east, or even ten. It might lie beyond a range of mountains, across a desert, or five hundred miles downstream. These challenges were accepted.

It was a country of challenge, of unbelievable difficulty, but it was also a land of beauty. It was not a land merely to be tasted. It was a land to be savored; even the storms had magnificence, and even the prairies had splendor. And it was the land that helped them to grow.

The plains seemed without limits, and the mountain ranges seemed impassable; where there was a trail, it was taken, and where there was none, one was built. Solutions to the problems encountered en route could be applied in settlements at the journey's end.

Where they walked there was opportunity, and where they rested there was anticipation. Often in their progress they made mistakes, but progress is built upon a foundation of error. Always the land lay wide about them, the vast sky overhead. There was no place for the poor in spirit, no place for the weak of heart. The white man learned much from the Indian that was not simply about living on and with the land: he learned to endure, to accept privation, to accept pain, not to whimper or cry aloud.

Men have changed the land, but the land has also changed men, and I hope *Frontier* can help the reader to understand some of the why and how of that process. It was the land of America that created Americans; what you read and see here is about our blood and our bone, and it is buried in the convolutions of our brains.

DISCOVERING AMERICA

The truth of the matter is that nobody wanted to discover America. Nobody was interested in a wild land sparsely inhabited by a Stone Age people. What they were looking for was Cathay and the Spice Islands. They wanted valuable merchandise they could sell in the Western world, and they wanted to get in and get out with a quick profit at the end of the voyage.

The story of the "discovery" of America is riddled with clichés that have been accepted virtually without question, most of which have no validity whatsoever.

Generations of schoolchildren have been taught that Europeans believed the world was flat and that if one sailed far enough one would fall off the edge. A few ignorant people may have believed this, but even the most stupid must have wondered why, if a ship could sail over the edge, the sea itself did not pour off into the void.

Anyone who has gone to sea has seen ships disappear over the horizon and has seen them with only topmasts visible, and for most this is proof enough that the world is round.

Most of those to whom Columbus went to sell his idea of sailing west to Cathay had no doubts; they were as well if not better informed than Columbus. Prince Henry the Navigator, of Portugal, knew about the shape of the earth, as did those who followed him. Common sense should have warned Columbus that the Portuguese, who controlled the route around Africa by which they hoped to reach the Indies would not welcome any such idea as his, which would open the way to all and destroy Portugal's monopoly.

Columbus was a striking figure of a man and a superb salesman. Moreover, his idea of sailing west to Cathay was a good one. The trouble was that he had grossly underestimated the size of the earth, following as he did the theories of Ptolemy.

Eratosthenes had, more than a thousand years before, estimated the circumference of the earth to within a few miles of its actual size, and whether those figures were available or not, many others had made estimates that far exceeded those of Ptolemy. Therefore, while those to whom Columbus presented his ideas did not need to be convinced the world was round, they did doubt his figures as to the length of the voyage ahead of him.

Columbus had what was to him convincing evidence. According to his son's account Columbus had spent a part of the year 1477 in Iceland, where he would have heard of "lands to the west." Moreover, during the period when Columbus was in Portugal, an officer in their navy was Coatlanen, from the island of Bréhat, in Brittany. The story is told in Brittany that it was Coatlanen who told Columbus about lands in the west long known to fishermen from Bréhat. Naturally Columbus would have believed those lands to be Cathay.

A fact often forgotten in writing of Columbus was that he married

page 12: Otter Coast, Acadia National Park, Maine.
page 13: Assateague Island National Seashore, Maryland-Virginia coast.
page 15: Live oak and palmetto in moving dune; Cumberland Island National
*   Seashore, Georgia.*

the daughter of Perestrello, a former governor of one of the Madeira Islands and himself a great seafaring man. From him Columbus acquired many charts and the story of the finding of the bodies, floating in the sea off the Azores, of two dark-skinned men with black hair and broad faces, resembling Asiatics.

All of this seemed to Columbus to substantiate his belief in the size of the earth as projected by Ptolemy and the length of the voyage to Cathay.

Another of the stories so often repeated and believed is that Queen Isabella pawned her jewels to finance Columbus. No doubt at one time she was prepared to do so, but it was simply not necessary. Most of the financing was done by Luis de Santangel and those associated with him. It was he who convinced Queen Isabella to authorize the voyage.

Before Columbus, Norsemen had made at least two dozen voyages to Greenland and North America, and there is considerable